DEVELOPING AFRICA THROUGH LOCAL CONTENT

The case of the Democratic Republic of Congo

Miguel Kashal Katemb

DEVELOPING AFRICA THROUGH LOCAL CONTENT

The case of the Democratic Republic of Congo

Preface by Olusegun Obasanjo

Afterword by Nana Addo Dankwa Akufo -Addo

L'Harmattan

5-7, rue de l'École-Polytechnique - 75005 Paris – France

Éditions L'Harmattan

ISBN : 978-2-336-64736-4
EAN : 9782336647364

Dedication

To His Excellency Mr. Félix Antoine TSHISEKEDI TSHILOMBO, President of the Democratic Republic of Congo, Head of State, bearer of a vision of economic emergence based on sovereignty and national dignity and initiator of Law No. 26/018 of June 30, 2026 on Local Content in the Democratic Republic of Congo.

I dedicate this work entitled *"The Development of Africa Through Local Content: The Case of the Democratic Republic of the Congo."*

This reflection is part of the continuation of the unfinished dream of the founding fathers of African independence, but also of the contemporary imperative for African leadership capable of transforming the continent's potential into shared prosperity.

Your Excellency Mr. President, Your commitment to economic sovereignty, the development of national resources, the promotion of Congolese entrepreneurship and the emergence of a strong and sustainable middle class and Congolese champions gives the local content policy a major strategic dimension.

Furthermore, Your Excellency's promulgation of Law No. 26/018 on local content on June 30, the anniversary of the independence of the Democratic Republic of Congo, was by no means a coincidence; you intended, I dare say, to perform a highly symbolic act, enshrining the idea that the political sovereignty acquired in 1960 must now be complemented by genuine economic sovereignty. Thus, on the very date on which the Congolese people won their political freedom, this same people now affirms its ambition to control its economic development, to enhance the value of its resources, and to guarantee the effective participation of Congolese citizens in the creation of national wealth.

Indeed, in a world where Africa remains an arena of geoeconomic rivalries between great powers, local content appears as a peaceful but determined weapon for regaining our autonomy, an instrument of social justice and a lever for industrialization.

By dedicating these pages to you, I pay tribute to the essential political will that must be embodied at the highest level of the Congolese State to make local content not merely an economic option, but a pillar of national sovereignty, productive discipline, and the dignity of the Congolese people.

May this work contribute, in its own modest way, to enriching strategic reflection for an Africa that produces, transforms, and consumes what it creates, and for a Democratic Republic of the Congo fully in control of its destiny.

With the highest consideration.

Miguel Kashal Katemb

Preface

Olusegun Obasanjo, Honorary President of the Federal Republic of Nigeria (1999-2007)

Olusegun Obasanjo

Agbe L'oba House, Quarry Road, Ibara
P.O. Box 2286, Abeokuta, Ogun State, Nigeria

2nd June 2026

Monsieur Miguel Kashal Katemb,
Kinshasa,
DRC.

My dear Kashal

Let me congratulate and commend you for your outstanding contribution to the ideas and concepts on local content in Africa which you have put in your book. I am delighted that you requested me to write the preface to the book, ***"The Development of Africa Through Local Content: The Case of the Democratic Republic of the Congo".***

Please find attached the approved version of the Preface for the publication. I would advise that the publication of the book should be of a high standard. I would like to have a personal copy in my personal library for reference and to add to my perspectives on the issue. I do hope that you will find time to visit Nigeria so that we can discuss more on the issue of local content and ither African development issues.

Please accept, Miguel, the assurances of my highest regards.

Your sincerely,

OLUSEGUN OBASANJO
(President of Nigeria, 1999-2007)

e-mail: obasanjonig@yahoo.com

PREFACE

It is with a deep interest in the economic future of our continent that I accepted to write the preface to the work of MiguelKashal Katemb.

Over the years, I have had the opportunity to observe his consistent commitment to the promotion of local content and the emergence of a stronger African entrepreneurship. His work is part of a dynamic that I have always considered essential: economic sovereignty through national control of value chains in significant areas of national economies in Africa.

Africa does not suffer from a lack of resources. Rather, it suffers from a deficit of local transformation, industrial discipline, and the proper structuring of its economic actors.

My experience as President of Nigeria convinced me that natural wealth, if not accompanied by proactive local content policies, can paradoxically coexist with widespread poverty. And the national policy must be locally-friendly, attractive, and sustained.

It was precisely to correct this contradiction that Nigeria undertook ambitious reforms over the past two decades and a half aimed at strengthening national participation in strategic sectors, particularly in the hydrocarbons sector.

When well designed and rigorously implemented, local content not only creates jobs and ensures wealth generation but it also builds sustainable national capital, promotes technology transfer, and strengthens economic sovereignty.

The book "The Development of Africa Through Local Content:The Case of the Democratic Republic of the Congo" fully aligns with this philosophy. It rightly reminds us that the challenge for African states is no longer simply to attract investment, but to intelligently anchor it locally so that the value created primarily benefits national economies while giving adequate returns on foreign investments.

Miguel Kashal Katemb highlights a fundamental truth: local content is neither a slogan nor an administrative posture. It isa strategic instrument for structural transformation. It requires regulatory rigor, institutional coherence, and above all, consistent political will, action, and monitoring.

What particularly distinguishes this work is its approach, which is simultaneously legal, economic, and operational. The author does not limit himself to a diagnosis; he proposes a structured vision of what an effective local content policy in the Democratic Republic of the Congo could look like a country whose mineral and human potentials are immense and must be put together for the development of the country in the first instance.

I remain convinced that Africa's future will largely depend on our collective ability to: strengthen the participation of local small and medium scale enterprises; invest in national skills; promote balanced partnerships with international investors; and build institutions capable of enforcing the rules of economic governance on sustainable development basis.

Miguel Kashal Katemb's career, at the crossroads of publicaction and entrepreneurial initiative, gives him particular legitimacy to convey this message. His commitment to a strong Congolese middle class and a competitive national private sector deserves recognition and applause.

In my view, this book represents far more than an academic contribution. It is a strategic reference document for African policy makers, regulators, investors, entrepreneurs and the youth of the continent.

May this reflection inspire bold public policies and encourage a new generation of African leaders and enterprenuers determined to make local content a genuine driver of shared prosperity and economic growth.

OLUSEGUN OBASANJO
President of the Federal Republic of Nigeria (1999-2007)
African Statesman

Prelude

What remains of the struggle of the 1960s, the struggle of "our fathers"? Pan-Africanism, Pan-Arabism, Africa The idea of unity, so dear to the former African leader Kwame Nkrumah, is it still shared by African youth and leadership today? Has the dream of "our fathers" remained a distant memory, an unattainable chimera? "Africa is the continent of the future," almost every analyst in the world keeps saying to the African continent.

Make America great " approach again " (to restore America's greatness) as well as the European ambition to maintain its strength, must also think about its future.

In his book, China-Africa, with its two evocative subtitles: "The Great Plunder...Chinese Dream, African Nightmare," journalist Julien Wagner offers a reflection, quoting an American columnist : *"In the midst of this competition already underway...Africa. Africa, for whom this 'dream' could well become the worst nightmare. As New York Times columnist Thomas Friedman stated, if the Chinese dream is indeed the same as the American dream, another planet is needed, since the former is underpinned by an eminently energy-intensive system. This is, moreover, one of its most obvious pitfalls, for it induces an insatiable and unsustainable appetite for raw materials; a morbid addiction often more destructive to others than to itself*[1]. " Such is the world today. The world in which Africa also wants to position itself.

One thing is clear in Africa today: the ideological struggles of the 1960s have been superseded by the necessity of economic development. Back then, you had to belong to one of two blocs: capitalist or socialist. Each bloc had its own economic model. Today, Africa must strive for greater economic integration

[1]Julien WAGNER : *China-Africa, the great plunder, Chinese dream, African nightmare?* Eyrolles Publishing, p. 13, 2014

among its 54 countries rather than getting bogged down in the outdated struggle of purely ideological positioning.

This is the challenge facing Africa tomorrow, or even Africa today, because despite possessing nearly half of the world's natural resources, Africa remains poor. Its human resources rank at the bottom of the global scale, according to the annual Human Development Index published by the United Nations Development Programme. In this context of a mix of challenges and potential for the "continent of the future," Africa must lift itself out of poverty by intelligently and strategically harnessing its resources.

In just a few years, Africa has gone from being a neglected continent (as it was considered for a time) to a region attracting all those with ambitions for greatness. Trade between Africa and China, India, Brazil, Russia, and even Turkey is growing. The United States is also getting involved, having already established a trade agreement with Africa.

How then can Africa simultaneously be a place of competition between great powers and profit from the exploitation of its resources?

A few years ago, addressing African youth through the youth of Ghana, President Barack Obama declared: " *The world will be what you make of it. You have the power to empower your leaders and build institutions that serve the people. You can serve your communities and contribute your energy and knowledge to create new wealth and new connections with the world. You can defeat disease, end conflict, and bring about change from the ground up.*" Barack Obama emphasized to African youth that they must now understand that "history is in the making." This history is that of African leadership creating wealth and change from the ground up, as the former US president stressed. This is the dream of African development through local content. "Africa is ready to take its part in the human adventure," say some experts on the continent. It must accelerate the industrialization of its economies by creating a circular and diversified economy around its raw materials. But more than the economic process,

Africa must work on its work ethic and the rigor of its people, because, as a popular saying in Asia, in particular, *states, the life of a nation lies in its culture*. This maxim is true for a nation, and it is also true for a continent. Yesterday, as today, and surely tomorrow, Africa faces the same reality: it constantly faces conquerors. But Africa must reinvent itself, break free from the cycle of repetition, which former French President Nicolas Sarkozy denounced nearly 20 years ago. *"The African peasant, who for millennia has lived in harmony with the seasons, whose ideal is to live in harmony with nature, knows only the eternal cycle of time, punctuated by the endless repetition of the same gestures and the same words... In this worldview where everything always begins again, there is no room for human adventure, nor for the idea of progress*," Nicolas Sarkozy had observed. He nevertheless proposed that Africa stop dwelling on the past, but learn from it in order to look to the future.

The dream of a prosperous Africa through local content necessarily and inevitably involves our understanding of the concept of work.

The concept of work, in the usual economic sense, is therefore the human activity that enables the production of goods and services. It remains clear that from gathering economies to the most elaborate division of labor, our societies are now deliberately perceived as work-oriented. But historically, Africa has been confronted with forced labor, often linked to forms of coercion, violence, or exploitation.

The example of ancient Greece shows us what was long lacking for work to acquire such a central place. The craftsman, and even more so the slave, could not conceive of himself as a producer of social value: his production was evaluated solely in terms of its use value and the value of the person for whom it was directly intended [1]. We therefore understand that this labor relationship would transform artisans into citizens. It is important to recall, in this regard, that the etymology of the word "work" contains the idea of torture (tripalium).

Political and social resistance movements emerged in Africa to fight against the colonial system and its oppressive practices, including forced labor. Political and social leaders such as Kwame Nkrumah in Ghana, Patrice-Emery Lumumba in the Democratic Republic of Congo, Jomo Kenyatta in Kenya, and Nelson Mandela in South Africa played a key role in the struggle against forced labor and colonial oppression. In short, Africans resisted the colonial model of forced labor in various ways, demonstrating their resilience, determination, and fight for justice and human dignity.

It was important, as a prelude to the developments that will follow, to evoke the concept of work because, I believe that, without a relationship to productive work free from all constraints, a relationship that makes work an instrument for the development of the African man, it would be illusory to believe in a dream of prosperity for Africa through the development of local content.

It is equally important to note that in the African conception of work, the notion of discipline is often neglected. Discipline is crucial in life because it allows one to achieve goals and improve productivity. It fosters the development of self-discipline, the ability to remain focused even in the face of discomfort, and the management of responsibilities. Discipline is a key element for personal and professional success, the establishment of healthy habits, and the maintenance of order, both in personal life and in society.

Respect for rules and standards is essential for the proper functioning of societies and institutions. Small-scale indiscipline can have negative consequences on a large scale and jeopardize any development project.

"Work, and after work, independence, my child; to be a burden on no one, that must be the motto of your generation." "Work ennobles man and ensures his independence." These famous quotes from the Ivorian writer Bernard Binlin Dadié on the importance of work for independence, although they are often cited without mentioning a specific work, but rather as a principle

of life that he advocated and which appeared in West African school textbooks, consecrates work as the pillar of dignity and independence.

Today, it is more crucial than ever not only to promote salaried employment but also, and above all, entrepreneurial work. This is work that creates wealth and added value, with the clear objective of growing local industry across all sectors. This is the essence of making local content development a true pillar of our dignity and independence, to paraphrase Bernard Dadie.

It is worth noting that the implementation of local content policies remains an undeniable factor in establishing social balance in a country.

Indeed, social equilibrium refers to a state of stability and harmony within a society, characterized by fairness in access to resources and opportunities (employment, care, housing), the satisfaction of everyone's basic needs, a fair distribution of wealth, and functional social relations, even if it may be theoretical in the face of structural inequalities, manifesting itself concretely in the balance between professional and personal life or the social mix of indigenous communities.

Recent history forcefully demonstrates that the success of local content policies is neither accidental nor a spontaneous market dynamic. It stems primarily from a political will embodied at the highest levels of government, translated into binding laws, asserted in the face of foreign interests, and defended in the name of national economic sovereignty.

In the United States, the famous Buy American Act was adopted as early as 1933 under President Herbert Hoover, requiring federal agencies to prioritize goods and services produced by American companies. This policy of national preference, far from being abandoned, has been strengthened under successive presidents, notably Donald J. Trump and Joe Biden, with the *Buy American, Hire American* and Inflation Reduction Act (2022), which makes access to public contracts, subsidies, and tax credits contingent on the use of local components and the employment of American labor. This policy has facilitated industrial relocation, the consolidation of domestic value chains, and the protection of strategic American industries. The United States now boasts 902 billionaires (according to the Forbes 2025 report), including Elon Musk, Jeff Bezos, Bill Gates, and Larry Ellison, to name just a few.

During the colonial period, India was heavily dependent on goods imported by Great Britain, which weakened its local economy and impoverished its people. Faced with this situation, Mahatma Gandhi developed an economic and political philosophy based on self-reliance and the development of local resources. He thus made local content, known as *" swadeshi, "* a cornerstone of his struggle for independence. We can then ask ourselves how Gandhi's thinking on local content constitutes a model for development and resistance.

For Gandhi, local content meant producing and consuming what was made in the country itself. He encouraged Indians to use local products, particularly khadi, a handwoven fabric. This practice valued the work of artisans and reduced economic dependence on foreign products. Swadeshi was therefore a form of economic self-sufficiency based on local resources and skills.

Gandhi's primary objective was economic liberation, an essential condition for political independence. By promoting local production, he sought to create jobs, especially in villages, and to combat poverty. Local content also had a moral dimension: he advocated simplicity, the dignity of manual labor, and solidarity. Consuming local products thus became an act of peaceful resistance against colonial domination.

Ultimately, Gandhi viewed local content as a crucial means of economic, social, and political liberation. Through swadeshi, he demonstrated that producing and consuming locally could strengthen a people's dignity and support more equitable development. His thinking remains relevant and serves as a source of inspiration for modern development and economic self-reliance policies.

Currently in India, the local content policy has been brought to the highest level of the State by Prime Minister Narendra Modi, through the " Make in India " doctrine, launched in 2014 and legally framed by Public Procurement. Order (Preference to Make in India). This regulation imposes mandatory thresholds for local added value on Indian public procurement, particularly in strategic sectors such as defense, energy, telecommunications, and infrastructure. Thanks to this proactive policy, India has developed a robust national industrial base, reduced its dependence on imports, and fostered the emergence of nearly 205 national champions who are billionaires (according to the Forbes 2025 report), including Mukesh Ambani, Gautam Adani, Ratan Tata, and Sunil Mittal, among many others capable of competing in global markets.

Gandhi's concept of local content pursued similar objectives of national development, but with different priorities than that conceived under Nelson Mandela in South Africa. However, the ultimate goal remained the redress of social inequalities, economic development, and the restoration of national dignity. The Black Economic Empowerment (or BEE/BBBEE) is a post-apartheid South African affirmative action policy aimed at correcting racial inequalities by integrating Black people into the economy through measures such as skills development, business ownership, and access to management. Its main objective is to redress the wrongs of apartheid by increasing the economic participation of historically disadvantaged groups. The local content policy was embraced at the highest levels of the post-apartheid state, particularly under the successive presidencies of Thabo Mbeki, Jacob Zuma, and Cyril Ramaphosa, through the legislative framework of the Broad- Based Black Economic Empowerment. The BBBEE Act and the Local Content Regulations applicable to public procurement and extractive industries. These legal instruments have enabled the strengthening of local businesses and a better redistribution of economic value to the benefit of South African nationals and the emergence of a black industrial bourgeoisie, the emblematic case of which is Patrice Motsepe, counted as a billionaire by Forbes 2025, and South Africa holds a continental record for the number of black millionaires, with 47% of the 37,800 black millionaires out of a total of 138,000 African millionaires listed.

In the People's Republic of China, local content has historically been the cornerstone of its power strategy. Under the leadership of Deng Xiaoping, and subsequently consolidated under the presidencies of Jiang Zemin, Hu Jintao , and now Xi Jinping, China has systematically imposed technology transfers, mandatory joint ventures, and the gradual integration of domestic companies into all industrial value chains. This strategy has been legally enshrined in several mechanisms, notably the Catalogue for the Guidance of Foreign Investment Industries and, more recently, the "Made in China 2025" plan, which explicitly aims for Chinese technological dominance in key sectors. The result is unequivocal: China has become the world's factory and a major technological power with approximately 516 billionaires (according to the Forbes 2025 report), including Hong Kong's Zhong Shanshan, Ma Huateng, Jack Ma (founder of Alibaba), Robin Zeng, and many others.

In Brazil, local content was established as a strategic pillar of industrial development under the presidency of Luiz Inácio Lula da Silva, particularly in the oil, gas, and shipbuilding sectors. Through Local Content Requirements integrated into Petrobras contracts and overseen by the National Petroleum Agency (ANP), Brazil imposed high quotas for local manufacturing, fostering the growth of domestic industry, the creation of skilled jobs, and technological expertise in deepwater offshore drilling. Thanks to this economic policy, Brazil boasts 56 billionaires (according to the Forbes 2025 report), including Jorge Paulo Lemann, Eduardo Saverin, Rubens Ometto, and André Esteves.

In Nigeria, former President Olusegun Obasanjo is often associated with local content, primarily as a political pioneer, even though formal legislation came after his presidency. Olusegun Obasanjo (president from 1999 to 2007) laid the political and institutional groundwork for local content, particularly in the oil and gas sector. He championed the idea that Nigerians should be major players in the exploitation of their natural resources, not just suppliers of unskilled labor. The "local value" strategy (in the sense of producing locally what was previously imported) fostered national industrial empires. On

Forbes Africa 2025, Nigeria produced more than four frequently cited billionaires, including Aliko Dangote, Mike Adenuga, Abdulsamad Rabiu and Femi Otedola.

In Ghana, the LI2204 law of 2013, or *Petroleum (Local Content and Local Participation) Regulations*, 2013, was promulgated in November 2013 under the presidency of John Dramani. Mahama is a fundamental regulation designed to maximize the use of Ghanaian labor, goods, and services in the oil and gas industry. It prioritizes local businesses and Ghanaian workers to promote technology transfer and require up to 30% local equity participation in companies within the sector. In 2020, under the presidency of Nana Akufo -Addo, the country strengthened the legal framework by enacting the new Minerals and Mining (Local Content and Local Participation) Regulations (LI 2431). *This regulation mandates that international mining companies source local goods and services, employ Ghanaians,* and facilitate skills transfer to maximize national economic impact and increase local business participation. As a result of these reforms, by 2025, Ghana will have a total of 2,600 millionaires, ranking it second in West Africa, after Nigeria, according to Africa Wealth Report, including Ibrahim Mouhammad, Ernesto Taricone, Charles Ampofo and many others.

In Zambia, local content policies have been built around a central objective: ensuring that the nation's mineral wealth primarily benefits Zambian citizens—a concept that can be described as a "local land content" approach. The first significant impetus came with the Citizens Economic Empowerment Act of 2006, adopted under the presidency of Levy Mwanawassa. Its strategic objective was to promote the participation of Zambian citizens in the economy, correct the historical dominance of foreign capital, and encourage joint ventures and national preference. This law laid the foundations for a moderate form of economic nationalism, notably by creating support mechanisms for local businesses. The decisive turning point, with the new wave of national sovereignty (2025), occurred under the presidency of Hakainde Hichilema. In 2025, Zambia adopted the Geological and Minerals Development (Local Content) Regulations (S.I.

No. 68 of 2025) which now impose, among other things: mandatory quotas for local purchases in the mining sector; a structured preference for companies owned by Zambians; and a progressive localization timetable (Key quotas: a minimum of 20% local goods and services from 2026 and a minimum of 40% within five years).

In the Democratic Republic of Congo, social inequalities are caused by imbalances deeply embedded in the society's social, economic, and political systems, creating systemic advantages and disadvantages for different social groups, limiting equitable access to resources and opportunities.

Before the advent of President Félix Tshisekedi, the legal framework already included some scattered sectoral mechanisms relating to local content and aimed, in a fragmented way, at promoting the integration of Congolese people into the economic life of the country.

This is notably the case with Law No. 16/010 of July 15, 2016, amending and supplementing Law No. 015-2002 on the Labor Code, which historically enshrined a principle of protecting the national workforce through priority hiring of nationals, regulation of the use of foreign labor, and the requirement of administrative authorization for the employment of expatriates. Following Law No. 18/001 of March 9, 2018, amending and supplementing Law No. 007/2002 of July 11, 2002, on the Mining Code , which introduced, in particular, the participation of Congolese citizens in the share capital (obligation to include Congolese individuals and workers in the capital of mining companies with a minimum threshold of 10% of the share capital, with 5% for Congolese individuals and 5% for other workers) ; Finally, Law No. 17/001 of February 8, 2017, establishing the rules applicable to subcontracting in the private sector, which constitutes the first legislation on the exercise of secondary activities in the value chain of the country's life, in that it provides for the exclusivity of subcontracting activities to companies with majority Congolese capital with a certification mechanism for eligible subcontractors; followed by the creation of the

Regulatory Authority for Subcontracting in the private sector, ARSP for short, as the regulatory structure;

These mechanisms, although relevant, have long remained ineffective and, moreover, are more focused on social and secondary activities, not on primary activities; lack a binding and robust sectoral monitoring mechanism; and show weak articulation with industrial policies.

The rise of President Félix Tshisekedi marks, in this respect, a decisive turning point towards a more systemic approach to economic sovereignty through local content. Indeed, public policy has gradually shifted from an essentially sectoral and social logic to a comprehensive and cross-cutting vision of local content, geared towards strengthening the economic independence of the Democratic Republic of Congo.

From this perspective, presidential action is part of a dynamic aimed at consolidating the Congolese middle class, with the ultimate goal of promoting and structuring a national entrepreneurial ecosystem capable of fostering the emergence of true Congolese economic champions (millionaires and billionaires). To this end, several legal reforms have been initiated to place Congolese citizens at the heart of national economic life, facilitating their transition from small-scale trade and secondary peripheral activities in value chains—particularly subcontracting—to greater participation in core activities, especially through access to share capital in companies operating in the private sector, particularly in strategic sectors such as mining, industry, telecommunications and digital technology, hydrocarbons, and infrastructure.

To implement this vision, the Congolese President promulgated Law No. 20/017 of November 25, 2020, concerning telecommunications and information and communication technologies. This law mandates the active participation of Congolese citizens in the share capital of licensed companies, up to 30%, distributed as follows: 25% for Congolese individuals and 5% reserved for the workforce. Furthermore, the promulgation of the local content law marks a major qualitative leap in consolidating national economic sovereignty by establishing appropriate mechanisms to guarantee the mandatory participation of Congolese citizens, both individuals and workers, in the capital of companies resulting from foreign investment, according to minimum thresholds defined by sector.

In the interest of structural efficiency, this orientation has been linked with the establishment of a national stock market (also supported by the draft Law on the organization and operation of a stock market in the Democratic Republic of Congo), through which Congolese individuals will also have access to the capital of companies operating in the national territory, by means of transparent mechanisms for the acquisition and disposal of shares.

The Local Content Law also establishes two Local Content Regulatory Authorities: one responsible for ensuring the coordination, harmonization, and consistency of all related issues in the private sector, and The other, for the same tasks, is in the public sector. This institutional innovation responds to the need to centralize and structure a system whose provisions were previously scattered across several sectoral texts.

These experiences converge on a universal truth: no nation has achieved sustainable development without protecting, structuring, and promoting its domestic economic actors. Local content is neither a favor nor archaic protectionism; it is a strategic weapon of sovereignty, embraced by major powers, but too often contested when claimed by Africa.

In the Democratic Republic of Congo, it was under his rule that President Felix-Antoine Tshisekedi Tshilombo initiated national local content policies to establish appropriate mechanisms to protect and promote training, capacity building and the use of local labor; mandatory use of local production (consume Congolese) and local supplies; transfer of technology and skills to nationals; use of national goods and services; mandatory participation of Congolese in the capital of private companies; access to markets and financing as well as the integration of nationals into the value chain of all sectors of the national economy in order to encourage the country towards sustainable development, economic growth and social balance.

Local content is an expression of the state's political will in economic matters. It reflects the strategic choice to move beyond the traditional conception of work, based primarily on wage labor, and to promote entrepreneurship as an engine of development. Through local content policies, the state encourages the transformation of workers into entrepreneurs capable of creating value, generating jobs, and strengthening the national economic fabric. This transition aims not only at the economic empowerment of the population, but also at reducing unemployment and consolidating inclusive and sustainable growth.

What needs to be clearly understood, and this is the main difference compared to previous regimes, is that the effectiveness and materialization of the local content implementation has only been achieved through the political will of the current President of the Republic, Félix Tshisekedi.

Introduction

The text I am presenting has as its touchstone the development of Africa through local content: the case of the Democratic Republic of Congo.

Several reasons justify these pages. What must be understood is that the dream of the struggle waged by the fathers of African independence in the 1960s, rooted in Pan-Africanism and Pan-Arabism, aimed at building a strong and economically and politically united Africa... seems a distant illusion for current generations. It will be even more so for future ones. And yet, Africa, with its potential, is a land of opportunity. It is as if the continent is held hostage between the Chinese and American dreams.

These lines pursue certain objectives. These pages aim to raise awareness that Africa constantly faces conquerors. These lines are a call for the essential and collective mobilization for a reinvention of Africa and a resolute commitment to its development.

Another objective, and one I believe is crucial, is to make Africans understand that developing local content is a true pillar of our dignity and independence, as well as an undeniable factor in establishing social equilibrium within a country. Indeed, it is about producing and consuming locally made goods and services.

This preference for local products allows us to value the work of artisans and reduce economic dependence on foreign goods. It involves training for economic self-sufficiency based on local resources and skills. As Gandhi so aptly observed, local content is an essential means of economic, social, and political liberation. Producing and consuming locally strengthens the dignity of a people and supports more equitable development.

Trade between Africa and China, India, Brazil, Russia, Turkey, the United States, and others is growing. How, then, can Africa simultaneously compete with major powers and benefit from the exploitation of its resources? In what ways and how can prioritizing local content serve as a model for development and resilience, guaranteeing African dignity and self-determination?

Some hypotheses have guided my thinking. Indeed, Africa is currently more preoccupied with the development and economic integration of its various countries than with the ideological struggles of the 1960s. As one can see, the African paradox lies in the gap between its diverse potential and its challenges, including the poverty of its population. My conviction is that Africa must lift itself out of poverty by intelligently and judiciously exploiting its resources.

Another hypothesis is that the dream of developing Africa through local content implies African leadership capable of creating wealth and change from the ground up.

My third hypothesis, for its development, is that Africa will have to accelerate the industrialization of its economies, creating a circular and diversified economy around its raw materials.

Furthermore, Africa's economic development requires, among other things, the promotion of discipline in the workplace and rigor among its stakeholders, given the profound impact culture has on a nation's life. Indeed, it would be illusory to believe in a dream of prosperity for Africa through the development of local content without valuing disciplined work. This discipline is essential for achieving objectives, improving productivity, fostering self-discipline, and managing responsibilities. It is crucial to understand that discipline guarantees respect for the rules and standards necessary for the proper functioning of a society.

Another conviction is that the success of local content policies stems from a political will embodied at the highest levels of government, expressed in binding laws, and supported by the idea of national economic sovereignty. The ultimate goal of promoting local content, in my view, is to redress social inequalities, foster economic development, and restore national dignity.

My final hypothesis is that a country's sustainable development depends on protecting, structuring, and promoting its national economic actors. Therefore, as I stated earlier, local content does not appear to me as a favor or a form of protectionism, but rather as a strategic weapon of sovereignty. Major powers have clearly understood this. Finally, it is essential to promote entrepreneurship as an engine of development.

Promoting local content as a foundation for development, dignity, and economic sovereignty is not unique to the Congo, but a universal awareness. Some countries have built their economies on the value of local content. I mentioned earlier Gandhi's India, China, South Africa, the USA, Brazil, and Nigeria, to name just a few.

I do not claim to have exhausted the debate on promoting local content to boost the Congolese economy. The contributions of others are useful and welcome to enrich the discussion.

My approach is reflective and critical, enriched by the research and experiences of others. A historical perspective has been essential in establishing my convictions.

The development of local content in Africa is intrinsically linked to work and discipline, but also, and above all, to the implementation of local content development policies. It is important to address the development challenges in general that Africa faces (Chapter I), as well as those specifically related to the efficient implementation of local content development policies in Africa (Chapter II), before discussing strategic approaches, the institutional framework, and the role of stakeholders in implementing local content development policies (Chapter III). Chapter IV outlines strategies for promoting local content in Africa, using the Democratic Republic of Congo as a case study. Chapter V focuses on the principles and mandatory guidelines for implementing sectoral and national local content development policies in the Democratic Republic of Congo. The final chapter examines the tools for developing local content and concludes with a general overview.

Chapter I

Current situation in Africa and development challenges

This first chapter focuses on the current situation in Africa and the challenges of development.
Indeed, for decades, Africa has posted sometimes enviable growth rates. Yet, this growth has not translated into industrialization, massive job creation, or a structural improvement in living conditions.
Why? Because this growth is extractive, extroverted, and dependent. Samir Amin, an Egyptian economist, explained this lucidly, saying that *"True development requires national control of strategic sectors and the local anchoring of the value created."*
Exporting raw materials while importing finished products amounts to externalizing wealth and internalizing poverty.
This chapter is structured around the following points: The first concerns the impact of globalization on local industries in Africa. The second presents the main development challenges facing Africa. The third point discusses some examples of local content on a global scale.

I. Impact of globalization on local industries in Africa

"Globalization, with its benefits and drawbacks, is above all a process that cannot be stopped, but whose direction depends in part on the political action that will be taken to control it," writes Pascal Lamy, former Director-General of the World Trade Organization, in the preface to the book entitled The World in 2025.
Pascal Lamy rightly predicted that the world in 2025 would have several centers of power and influence. The former head of the WTO foresaw *"the almost certain emergence of a multipolar world in which three main blocs centered around the United States, the European Union, and Asia will be in competition."* The interaction,

whether positive or negative, between these centers of power would inevitably have an impact on the African continent. To understand the idea expressed by Lamy, one need only look at and analyze two events that shook the global economy: two years of the Covid-19 pandemic and three years of war in Ukraine truly reshaped the world. How can we explain and make a farmer in MASIMANIMBA, in the Kwilu province, in the west of the Democratic Republic of Congo, understand that the bread he buys from the bakery will now only cost him twice as much as before, because of the shortage of wheat flour which is no longer coming due to the war in Ukraine?

On February 24, 2022, the war that broke out between Russia and Ukraine sent more refugees fleeing than the European continent had seen since the collapse of Nazi Germany. The conflict triggered a global energy crisis. It revived the specter of food shortages. It disrupted global supply chains. It accelerated soaring inflation and generated cascading social tensions.

These events may be taking place nearly 10,000 kilometers away, but the shockwaves are being felt even in places where Ukraine has never been heard of. The global economy is globalized. There's no need to resort to complex economic theories to explain this phenomenon. It's all happening right before our eyes.

Similarly, the experience of the Coronavirus (Covid-19) pandemic was equally rich in lessons. Companies in Africa had to close their operations, lay off staff, or downsize to cope with the economic crisis triggered by the health crisis that emerged in China in 2020.

Africa facing the world

Although it accounts for less than 5% of global trade, the African continent remains a link in the global economic chain. A weak link, yes. But a link nonetheless. Africa does not directly influence the course of the global economy, but it remains an element of the system. Its natural resources (which we will discuss) represent a potential source of soft power for the continent. It must be said that the debate on Africa's true place is not entirely settled. Twenty years ago (in 2005), Nicole Gnesotto and Giovanni Grevi observed that *"debates on the situation and prospects of the African continent are most often marked by two opposing scenarios: Afro-pessimism and*

Afro-optimism. According to the former, Africa will remain a continent ravaged endemically by poor governance, corruption, violence, poverty, drought, and disease." Conversely, the optimistic hypothesis predicts that unprecedented opportunities will arise, particularly thanks to a new generation of African leaders ready to address the continent's problems and support its integration into the globalization process.

In other words, this optimism is based on the idea of birth rates and intergenerational succession. Indeed, generations succeed one another due to the inevitable birth and death inherent in the human condition. Therefore, African leaders are no exception to this rule. Thus, optimism for a new and better change remains possible, with new leaders.

The lines below outline the main development challenges facing Africa.

II. Presentation of the main challenges facing Africa in terms of development

Africa is a multifaceted continent with diverse challenges. To study this continent, or rather its main challenges, it is necessary to approach it holistically. The African continent is the poorest of all continents. Unemployment is endemic there. But instead of viewing these facts as isolated entities, a sound analysis must consider economic phenomena as a whole. Economic phenomena are always interconnected: education levels or workforce quality, national income, employment, unemployment, investment, savings, and so on.

Some analysts believe that Africa is in a state of permanent underproduction and that the state, which is responsible for intervention, is often itself powerless. According to John Maynard Keynes's theory, the state, through its intervention, "is able to restore fundamental balances."

Therefore, the main challenges for Africa's development concern the education sector, unemployment, economic growth, poverty and inequality, governance and institutions, climate change and the environment.

II.1. Education

"Is there still a need to question the interrelationships between population, education, and development, and more specifically, the crucial role played by education, a role that seems self-evident?" asks Marc Pilon in the introduction to his scientific study entitled *Challenges of Development in Sub-Saharan Africa: Education at Stake*. Here, he is referring to "school" education, that which is transmitted through educational institutions, and not the education traditionally provided by families and communities. Marc Pilon continues: "One of the synthesis reports published for the 36th session of the UN Commission on Population and Development held in 2003, which addressed this very theme, reminds us that the international community has explicitly recognized that education, particularly primary education, is essential for social and demographic progress, sustainable economic development, and gender equality."

Political and governance bodies in Africa have placed quality education among the Sustainable Development Goals (SDG 4). According to the African Union's 2022 Sustainable Development Report, progress in quality education across Africa has been slow. The COVID-19 pandemic has reversed some of the progress made by African countries in recent years. Despite significant progress in school enrollment, approximately 288 million school-age children are still not in school, particularly in conflict-affected countries. "In 2021, proficiency levels for children in Africa (excluding North Africa) in second or third year of primary school were estimated at 28.9% for mathematics and 17.82% for reading. These rates are below the global average of 62.6% for mathematics and 61.4% for reading." One unfortunate fact remains: most African countries continue to allocate less than 20% of their national budget to education. The quality of education, or the quality of teaching, is also compromised by inadequate school infrastructure and a lack of qualified teachers. In his book, * *Higher and University Education in Congo-Kinshasa: Challenges and Ethics**, *Leon Matangila Musadila explains* that the challenges, particularly in the education sector in the DRC, stem from the inadequacy of school curricula, which remain ill-suited to local and unique realities. The decline in academic standards is increasingly evident due to the disconnect between curricula and lived experience. The precarious living conditions of teachers do not always foster genuine motivation or the expected results. This impacts the quality of students' education. The challenges become even greater for these students when they begin secondary and university studies. The modest wages, living and working conditions often lead to demands, strikes and the elasticity of school and academic years (Léon Matangila, *Higher and university education in Congo-Kinshasa, challenges and ethics,* Paris, L'Harmattan, 2003).

In this specific respect, the Democratic Republic of Congo serves as a model case, as since President Félix Tshisekedi came to power, several programs have been implemented nationwide, notably free primary education and the Local Development Program for the 145 Territories (PDL-145T), which includes the construction of school infrastructure. The Congolese head of state stated before the UN General Assembly in September 2024 that free basic education had enabled nearly 4 million children to attend school in five years.

Several countries have used the quality of education as a lever to escape underdevelopment. Jean Ortiz and Georges Fournial explain how Cuba relied on the "education revolution" to set itself on the path to development. "If there is one area where Cuba has achieved spectacular successes worldwide, it is education. The majority of its population has now reached the 'sixth grade,' the equivalent of the former primary school leaving certificate, and the average level of education is also high... The country can proudly boast of these victories over ignorance... All Cuban school-aged children go to school... Do we fully appreciate what this means in terms of effort, resources invested, and therefore future prospects in a small country that is beginning to emerge from underdevelopment?" ask Jean Ortiz and Georges Fournial .

What needs to be understood is that unemployment is a real challenge to a country's economic takeoff.

II.2. Unemployment

According to the International Labour Organization (ILO), the labor market in Africa faces increasing challenges, particularly due to the

growing demographics of the working-age population, which continues to lead to disillusionment among young people, pushing them to abandon their efforts to find employment. According to ILO data, the working-age population in Sub-Saharan Africa increased by 53 million people between 2019 and 2023. The organization estimates that in 2023, 25.9% of young people will be classified as NEET (Not in Education, Employment, or Training), meaning they are neither in education, training, nor employed. These figures represent an increase compared to the rate of 22.2% recorded in 2013. Yet, we are talking about the continent that everyone is vying for because of its immense natural resources.
Africa is therefore suffering from "the Dutch disease," the greatest contemporary danger, notes Julien Wagner. The author of the book *China Africa: The Great Plunder, Chinese Dream, African Nightmare? * first explains what the concept of "Dutch disease" refers to. "This pathology takes its name from its first theorized occurrence following the sudden loss of competitiveness experienced by the Netherlands in the 1960s. This affliction, better known today as the 'resource curse,' has been spreading like an epidemic ever since. It affects countries that discover they are rich in natural resources. This good fortune, if poorly managed, can turn into a 'curse' under the combined effect of a sharp appreciation of the national currency and over-specialization in one sector at the expense of manufacturing industries (this is what happened to the Netherlands after gas reserves were discovered in the province of Groningen and in the North Sea)." Numerous examples illustrate this assertion. “The exploitation and subsequent export of abundant oil, gas, or mineral resources triggers an influx of foreign currency, which suddenly and significantly increases the value of the national currency. However, this appreciation harms all other export-oriented economic sectors by increasing the price of the products sold. Simultaneously, the highly profitable exploitation of raw materials attracts all the country's capital. This effect disproportionately shifts investments and literally drains other industries. The fortunate holder of this wealth will soon find themselves trapped in a vicious cycle, condemned to exclusive dependence on a single sector of activity which, to make matters worse, requires little labor and is therefore a weak job creator. This is the risk of economic rent-seeking. And in Africa, it is no longer

an epidemic that threatens, but an endemic one. In about twenty years, the continent has become the new Eldorado of raw materials." "According to various estimates, it could hold between a third and half of the planet's natural resource reserves. In Equatorial Guinea, Ghana, South Sudan, Nigeria, Angola, Mozambique, Tanzania, Zimbabwe, the Republic of Congo, the Democratic Republic of Congo, and other African countries, new gas, oil, or precious metal deposits are discovered every year. And that's not counting the new explorations undertaken in previously neglected areas like Somalia. A goldmine? It all depends on who's at stake."

South Africa, China's largest African trading partner, is one of the world's most mineral-rich countries. Yet, it suffers from an unemployment rate close to 40% of its working-age population. Its industrial sector is struggling, and its income disparities make it one of the most unequal countries in the world. This situation clearly stems from the enormous revenues generated in the mining sector, which foster a rentier economy. Zambia, one of the African countries with the closest ties to Beijing, also faces a similar vicious cycle, albeit on a much larger scale. In this southern African nation, copper alone accounts for nearly 80% of exports. How, under such conditions, can one believe in sustainable future development?

Even if China pays for its copper with hospitals and roads, once the copper runs out, the country will find itself without industry, without a job-creating sector, and with infrastructure it can no longer afford to maintain. Despite growth exceeding 5% for more than a decade thanks to soaring copper prices, life expectancy in Zambia (49 years in 2011 according to the UNDP[3]) and its Human Development Index (the country ranked 163rd out of 169 in 2012) remain among the lowest in the world. In Nigeria, Africa's leading crude oil producer, the oil boom has consumed the entire economy: 95% of its foreign exchange earnings and 80% of its budget revenue come from oil sales alone. And at the same time, a large majority don't see a single drop of it," argued Julien Wagner in his aforementioned book.

In addition to this development, unemployment is also caused by rural exodus and urban overpopulation. The concentration of the population, especially young people, in large cities, and the abandonment of the countryside inevitably leads to joblessness.

In addition to unemployment, I must point out economic growth as a real challenge to be met.

II.3. Economic growth

Many African countries have experienced sustained economic growth in recent years, although this growth has been uneven across countries and regions. Some countries have succeeded in diversifying their economies and attracting foreign investment, while others face structural economic challenges. The pages below allude to poverty and inequality as challenges to development.

II.4. Poverty and inequalities

Despite economic progress, poverty and inequality remain major challenges in Africa. A large portion of the African population still lives in poverty, with limited access to education, healthcare, and other basic services. Now, it is important to discuss governance and institutions.

II.5. Governance and institutions

Governance and institutions in Africa remain a major challenge to development. Corruption, lack of transparency, and political instability can hinder economic and social progress in many African countries.
What needs to be clearly seen is that it is imperative to take climate change and the environment into account.
II.6. Climate change and the environment

Africa faces increasing challenges related to climate change, such as drought, floods, and environmental degradation. These challenges have significant repercussions for food security, public health, and the sustainability of natural resources in Africa.

In summary, Africa faces complex and interconnected development challenges that require a holistic approach. Strengthening the capacities of local actors, promoting transparent and accountable governance, investing in education and health, fostering economic diversification, and adapting to the challenges of climate change are essential. International cooperation, public-private partnerships, and citizen engagement are also key elements in supporting sustainable development in Africa. By working together and adopting innovative approaches, Africa can overcome its current challenges and move towards a more prosperous and inclusive future for all. What examples of local content should be considered globally?

III. Local Content : Examples on a Global Level

One thing is clear in Africa: the continent is rich in natural resources. These resources represent an asset that creates opportunities. When natural resources are managed effectively, they generate wealth. Extractive resources, through their market value, can accelerate Africa's economic transformation by creating jobs and opportunities for current and future generations. In Africa, as elsewhere, one of the challenges facing resource-rich countries, particularly in the extractive sector, is how to maximize profits from the extractive industry. Local content policies potentially offer countries and communities an effective path. But as we have already stated, local content policies are not a magic bullet. They require regular monitoring and intelligent coordination to meet a country's expectations. Many resource-rich countries are increasingly introducing local content policy requirements through laws, regulations, contracts, and tendering practices. Several experiences have demonstrated the positive impact of local content policies, but there are also cases where success is less evident. Research and analysis have shown that local content objectives are often not met and opportunities are missed due to inadequate implementation of local content policies.

Local content, comparative table of examples from elsewhere

FRANCE vs USA

DEFINITION AND LEGAL FRAMEWORK

• Local content is often addressed in the context of public procurement, industrial policy, and calls for tenders. • There are no strict regulations imposing a minimum percentage of local content in all sectors. • Local content is encouraged more through preference criteria in public procurement or sectoral policies (e.g., aeronautics, energy). • France also applies European rules that limit discrimination based on nationality in public procurement (European single market principle).	• Local content is heavily regulated by federal laws, notably the Buy American Act (1933), which requires federal agencies to purchase products manufactured in the United States. • There is also the Berry Amendment in the defense sector, which requires the use of American materials and products in military contracts. • The United States takes a more protectionist approach to local content, with clear and often restrictive requirements.

SECTORS OF APPLICATION

• The concept of local content is often sector-specific and less rigid, favoring strategic sectors such as aeronautics, energy (particularly renewables), and infrastructure. • The policy aims to support French SMEs, but in compliance with European competition rules.	• Local content is applied in several key sectors: defense, infrastructure, energy, manufacturing, transportation. • The approach is more systematic, based on federal laws and specific eligibility criteria. 1

MECHANISMS AND INCENTIVES

• Use of preferential clauses in public tenders (selection criteria favoring bids with more local content) • Industrial and innovation support programs to strengthen local capabilities	

SOUTH AFRICA vs NIGERIA

LEGAL FRAMEWORK

South Africa	Nigeria
• There are laws and policies encouraging the use of local suppliers, especially in the mining, energy, and manufacturing sectors. • One important policy is B-BBEE (Broad-based black economic empowerment), which aims to promote the economic participation of black South Africans, often linked to the use of local content.	• Nigeria has very strict local content legislation, particularly in the oil and gas sector: the Nigeria Oil and Gas Industry Content Development Act (2010). • This law imposes specific rules to ensure a high proportion of local labor, materials, and services in projects.

CONCERNED SECTORS

South Africa	Nigeria
• Mining, energy, construction, telecommunications, manufacturing. • Local content is often linked to social inclusion (B-BBEE).	• Mainly oil and gas, but also energy, construction, and telecommunications. • The oil sector is the most regulated to ensure local content.

REQUIREMENTS

South Africa	Nigeria
• Variable percentage of local content depending on the sector (e.g., often around 60-70%) • Companies must also meet B-BBEE criteria.	• Very clear and strict requirements, often a minimum of 70% local content in oil contracts. • Obligation to employ local labor and use local materials and services.

CONTROL AND IMPLEMENTATION

South Africa	Nigeria
• Public contracts include local content clauses. • B-BBEE is an important criterion for accessing markets.	• The Nigerian Content Development and Monitoring Board (NCDMB) supervises and controls the implementation of local content rules. • Companies often have to obtain

Of course! Here is a simple and clear comparison of local content practices between Morocco and Egypt.

MOROCCO vs EGYPT

LEGAL FRAMEWORK

Morocco	Egypt
• Morocco encourages local content, especially in the industrial, automotive, aerospace, and renewable energy sectors. • There are policies to promote local suppliers and develop national skills, but without very strict laws as in Nigeria.	• Egypt has put in place regulations to promote local content, particularly in oil and gas, as well as in infrastructure. • The law often requires a minimum percentage of local content in public contracts, but this varies depending on the sector.

CONCERNED SECTORS

Morocco	Egypt
• Automotive, aerospace, renewable energy, manufacturing, construction. • The focus is on industrial development and exports.	• Oil and gas, construction, energy, manufacturing. • Strong focus on the energy sector

REQUIREMENTS

Morocco	Egypt
• No single mandatory percentage, but contracts favor the use of local products and services • Companies are encouraged to train and employ Moroccan skills	• Often a minimum of 40% to 60% local content in certain projects, particularly in oil and gas. • Requirement to use local suppliers and develop the local workforce

MONITORING AND ENFORCEMENT

Morocco	Egypt
• Enforcement is mainly through public tenders and incentives for local investment. • No specific agency dedicated to monitoring local content	• Public authorities supervise compliance, particularly in major infrastructure and energy projects • Public contracts include specific clauses on local content

Promoting local content requires adopting models rooted in the economic and social realities of African countries. Notable examples include the Republic of Congo, Guinea, and Ethiopia.

- The Republic of the Congo

The 1968 Establishment Convention between the Republic of Congo and oil operators stipulates that: *"The operator undertakes to use as a priority companies or enterprises established in Congo provided that their prices, qualities, quantities, delivery and sales conditions compared to supplies available abroad do not make them more expensive."*

In this Central African country, the Hydrocarbons Code also governs the issue of companies incorporated under Congolese law. Article 22 of the Hydrocarbons Code of August 23, 1994, requires oil companies to give priority, for the execution of work necessitated by their activities, to the supplies and services of companies incorporated under Congolese law, provided that the conditions of price, deadlines, and quality are substantially equivalent. Article 9 of Law No. 3-2000 of February 1, 2000, concerning the conditions for subcontracting in the Congo, stipulates that: *"The main contractor shall, whenever possible, give priority for subcontracting contracts to companies incorporated under Congolese law, promoted and managed by Congolese nationals, and whose technical and management staff is comprised of at least 60% Congolese nationals."* In these companies, "a minimum 30% shareholding in the capital of the subcontracting companies shall be reserved for Congolese nationals."

These provisions are reinforced by Articles 3 and 4 of Decree 2000-180 of August 7, 2000, regulating subcontracting in the oil sector, which stipulates that *"only companies or firms whose registered office or authorized legal representative is in Congo may engage in subcontracting* ," and that, with equal technical capacity and financial conditions as assessed by the approval committee, priority for subcontracting contracts is given to companies incorporated under Congolese law, particularly those promoted and managed by Congolese nationals and whose technical and management staff is comprised of at least 60% Congolese nationals. The following paragraphs discuss the case of Ethiopia.

• Ethiopia

In Ethiopia, local content is a strategic priority, particularly in key sectors such as manufacturing and mining, with the aim of boosting economic growth and reducing dependence on imports.
Ethiopia's new industrial policy prioritizes local manufacturers to strengthen the sector. The goal is to replace more than 96 imported products with locally manufactured alternatives within the next three years. The government has facilitated access to credit for the manufacturing sector to address financing challenges. In April 2024, the government eased regulations to allow foreign investors to participate in wholesale and retail trade, while requiring them to purchase local products, such as coffee, to boost exports. In the mining sector, mining license holders are required to give preference to Ethiopian goods and services of comparable quality and available in a timely manner. Only Ethiopian nationals are permitted to conduct reconnaissance operations and obtain licenses for artisanal mining.
The government is offering incentives to mining companies that promote the use of domestic resources.
In the energy sector, electricity production is open to foreign investors, but transmission and distribution via the integrated national grid are reserved for domestic investors.
Although there are no specific requirements for local equity participation in power projects, the Investment

Act and general regulations mandate local participation or joint ventures in certain sectors.
In the agricultural sector, a pillar of the economy and the main source of income for Ethiopia, the government is seeking to attract investment in agribusiness to strengthen local production. The country has fertile land and a climate favorable to the production of diverse crops, offering investment opportunities in cotton, livestock, fruits, vegetables, and grains. I will discuss the Republic of Guinea in the next section.

• The Republic of Guinea

Guinea's local content law (Decree L-2024-013-CNT of April 24, 2024) establishes rules to promote the participation of Guinean businesses and personnel in projects in Guinea, particularly in the mining sector. An independent Local Content Regulatory Authority (ARCL), tasked with overseeing project compliance, penalizing violations, and managing disputes, has even been created.
The law also emphasizes the use of local staff with specific quotas and gives preference to Guinean suppliers and service providers, with the following main objectives:

- Priority to local employment: The law imposes minimum hiring quotas for Guinean staff, which evolve over time for management and supervisory positions;
- Encouraging local businesses: This aims to promote the integration of Guinean businesses, particularly SMEs, into value chains;
- Technology transfer: The law encourages the transfer of know-how and technologies to Guinean personnel;
- Preference for Guinean service providers and suppliers for goods and services;
- Promoting the use and sharing of infrastructure between different projects and with the State.

The Regional Content Regulatory Authority (ARCL) oversees local content, ensures project compliance, imposes sanctions, and publishes reports on policy implementation. Non-compliance may result in administrative and civil penalties, including fines, contract terminations, license withdrawals, and project suspensions.
Although the new law could have a significant impact on costs, partner selection and business continuity for mining and other companies, local content is seen as a lever for sustainable economic development and benefits for all stakeholders.

Conclusion

This first chapter focused on the current situation in Africa and the challenges of development. It was organized into three points.

The first focuses on the impact of globalization on local industries in Africa. Indeed, the globalized economy has led to diverse feelings: Afro-pessimism for some, and hope for others, which rests on the succession of new leaders.

The second speaker addressed the main challenges facing Africa in terms of development. Among the challenges to Africa's economic development, I mentioned education, unemployment, economic growth, poverty and inequality, governance and institutions, climate change, and the environment.

The third point was based on several examples of local content worldwide, including the Republic of Congo, Guinea, and Ethiopia. Experiences from various countries show that local content becomes a lever for economic sovereignty when supported by clear policies, public-private partnerships, and monitoring mechanisms. It is important to understand that there are challenges to implementing local content development policies in Africa, as I will explain in the following chapter.

Chapter II

The challenges to the efficient implementation of local content development policies in Africa

Beyond the African approach to the concept of work and development issues in general, the development of local content in Africa faces several challenges that hinder its full realization. These challenges include: a lack of technical and technological capacity, inadequate infrastructure, limited access to financing, international competition, a complex regulatory and administrative framework, weak local demand, and the need to strengthen local capacities.

I. Lack of technical and technological capabilities

Local industries in Africa can often lack the technical and technological skills needed to produce high-quality, competitive local content for the global market.

Indeed, African companies generally lack the knowledge, skills or experience necessary to accomplish certain tasks, particularly those related to new technologies.

Several factors can explain a lack of technical capacity:

- Rapid technological evolution: Current employee skills often become obsolete due to the accelerating pace of technological progress, particularly in areas such as artificial intelligence.
- Talent shortage: The labor market does not offer enough qualified candidates to meet the demand for certain specialized technical skills.

- Weakness in continuing education: most companies do not invest enough in the training and skills development of their staff.

  A lack of technical capacity can have serious consequences:

- Decreased productivity and quality: Work is often slowed down, errors more frequent because employees do not master the necessary tools and methods.
- Loss of competitiveness: companies are unable to innovate or adapt to market changes because their teams are not trained in new technologies.
- Additional costs: Recruiting qualified staff and providing the necessary training to address skills gaps generates significant expenses.

  To address technical skills gaps, several strategies can be adopted:

- Internal capacity building:
  - Training and workshops: Offer regular training to enable employees to acquire new skills.
  - Coaching and mentoring: Enabling experienced employees to share their knowledge and mentor newer employees.
- Targeted recruitment:
  - Hiring freelancers: Calling on external experts for specific projects to quickly provide precise skills.
  - Recruiting new talent: Searching for candidates with the missing technical skills.

    The biggest regret is the inadequacy of the infrastructure, as I point out in the following lines.

II. Inadequate Infrastructure

Communication, energy, and transport infrastructure can be inadequate or unreliable in many parts of Africa, making it difficult to produce and distribute local goods. This deficit, caused by a lack of reliable and sufficient infrastructure, affects the quality of life, economic growth, and efficiency of businesses that rely on these networks to operate.

Limited or unreliable ICT networks hinder the production, distribution and marketing of local products online and offline.

Electricity shortages and frequent outages make production expensive and difficult, as businesses and creators lack a stable energy source.

Deficient transport infrastructure complicates the physical distribution of local products and the mobility of people, thus limiting the reach and impact of local production.

Inadequate infrastructure, combined with political and funding problems, is hindering the development of the local creative industry and the economy in general.

Initiatives such as the Programme for Infrastructure Development in Africa (PIDA) aim to mobilize the resources needed to modernize the continent's infrastructure.

To enhance connectivity, stimulate economic growth and support the development of local content, targeted investments in transport, energy and ICT infrastructure are essential.

Infrastructure needs include the modernization of transport networks (roads, railways, ports, airports), the provision of reliable electricity (power plants, distribution networks) and the development of ICT (telecommunications networks, fiber optics, digital infrastructure such as data centers) to guarantee reliable and efficient internet connectivity.

Major obstacles include financial challenges, lack of long-term planning, governance issues, political instability, and regulatory rigidities that hinder private investment and efficiency.

Funding for major projects is often insufficient, and private investment is hampered by perceived risks, inefficiencies, and unstable regulatory frameworks.

Several regulatory and political obstacles can be identified, including:

- Complex or unstable regulatory frameworks, vague regulations or regulations subject to frequent changes, which discourage investment.
- Governance problems, mismanagement, corruption and lack of transparency hinder the planning and implementation of projects.
- Cumbersome administrative procedures related to land acquisition, obtaining permits and other authorizations are often lengthy and expensive.

Some obstacles, however, are structural in nature; these include, among others:

- Lack of long-term planning: absence of coherent infrastructure plans leading, in the long term, to an inefficient allocation of resources.
- Limited institutional capacity: Institutions responsible for planning and managing infrastructure often lack the necessary resources and expertise.
- Problems accessing financing: Lack of access to long-term financing on favorable terms is a major obstacle, particularly for developing countries. The following sections address limited access to financing.

III. Limited access to financing

Local businesses in Africa may face difficulties in obtaining adequate financing to develop and promote their products. This lack of financial support can be a major obstacle to the development of local content.

Limited access to finance for businesses is a problem caused by a lack of reliable information, the limited risk appetite of financial institutions, legal and regulatory shortcomings, and credit rationing

. This problem hinders business growth and innovation, particularly for SMEs, and leads to lost investment and jobs.

Solutions include expanding financing instruments, using digital technologies, and improving legal and tax frameworks.

Banks often struggle to assess the viability of businesses due to a lack of transparency and reliable information. They frequently refuse to grant loans, even at high interest rates, because of the perceived high risk associated with these businesses.

Financial institutions are reluctant to take risks, especially with small and medium-sized enterprises, particularly because of internal management and governance problems that make SMEs less attractive to lenders.

Certain categories of entrepreneurs, such as women and young people, face additional difficulties in accessing financing.

Consequences: growth is hampered because companies do not have the necessary funds to invest, expand and create jobs; the inability to innovate and invest leads to a loss of competitiveness in the market; a large number of companies cannot access basic financial services, which keeps them in the informal sector or puts them at a disadvantage, thus creating a kind of financial exclusion.

Several solutions are proposed, including:

- Diversification of financial instruments:

  Offer a wider range of financing products beyond traditional bank loans, such as venture capital, bond issues, and crowdfunding solutions.

- Improving the business environment:

  Establish more robust legal and regulatory frameworks and effective bankruptcy systems.

- The use of digital technologies:

  Leveraging technology to reduce transaction costs and expand access to financial services.

- Government support:

Implement public guarantees, improve the payment system and accelerate payments for public contracts to SMEs.

- Strengthening cooperation:

  Encourage synergies between the public and private sectors, for example through mutual guarantee companies to share risks.

  What needs to be understood is that local businesses face international competition, including multinationals and foreign companies.

III.International competition

Local businesses in Africa often face fierce competition from multinationals and foreign companies that dominate global markets. This competition can make it difficult for local businesses to grow and promote their products.

Multinational corporations can use internationalization strategies to reduce production costs and improve the competitiveness of their products and services, making it difficult for local businesses to compete. Furthermore, challenges such as limited access to finance, poor infrastructure, and unstable political and regulatory environments can hinder the development of local businesses.

Multinationals are crowding out local competition by reducing their production costs and taking advantage of cheaper labor in some African countries, thereby improving their price competitiveness.

They can also influence consumer purchasing behavior by improving non-price competitiveness, that is, through strategies such as improving the quality of products or services.

Multinationals also use the internationalization strategy which consists of acquiring critical mass and financial capacity to dominate the market, access major accounts, and spread their risks across several geographies.

The complexity of the regulatory and administrative framework should be noted in the following point.

IV. Complex regulatory and administrative framework

Regulations and administrative procedures in Africa can sometimes be complex and poorly adapted to the needs of local industries. This can hinder the development of local content by creating bureaucratic and legal obstacles.

This problem manifests itself in several forms that create bureaucratic and legal barriers for local businesses.

In some countries, there is a lack of clear political vision to guide industrialization, which is reflected in ineffective or inconsistent regulations.

Policies to protect local industry are often not applied consistently, thereby weakening African businesses in the face of international competition.

Some administrative procedures are poorly adapted to local realities, creating obstacles to the registration, management and development of businesses, particularly for small and medium-sized enterprises (SMEs).

Administrative red tape and red tape are notorious problems that slow down processes and discourage entrepreneurs.

And above all, a lack or poor coordination between different public institutions makes procedures long and complex for businesses, promotes corruption and increases costs for businesses by creating an uncertain business environment.

Consequences for local content

- Additional costs: Bureaucratic obstacles increase the costs and duration of procedures, which penalizes the competitiveness of local businesses.
- Limitation of investments: The difficulty of navigating the regulatory framework may discourage investors, including local ones, from engaging in the development of the industry.

- Weak industrial linkages: Local content policies may be poorly designed or ineffective, failing to foster partnerships between extractive companies and local suppliers.

The following solutions should be considered:

- Regulatory reforms: reviewing legal instruments to adapt them to local realities and support industrialization.
- Simplifying procedures: Developing clear procedure manuals and implementing more efficient management systems will help simplify processes for businesses.
- Better governance: Strengthening governance and public institutions to contribute to a more transparent and favorable economic environment.

Multi-stakeholder approach: Developing local content requires a collaborative approach involving government, the private sector, citizens, and businesses, with clearly defined roles and responsibilities.

- Regulatory reforms: reviewing legal instruments to adapt them to local realities and support industrialization.
- Simplifying procedures: Developing clear procedure manuals and implementing more efficient management systems will help simplify processes for businesses.
- Better governance: Strengthening governance and public institutions to contribute to a more transparent and favorable economic environment.
- Multi-stakeholder approach: Developing local content requires a collaborative approach involving government, the private sector, citizens and businesses, with clearly defined roles and responsibilities.

It is also important to highlight the weak local demand in the following point.

A) Low local demand

In some cases, there may be low demand for local content due to a preference for foreign products or the perception that local content is of lower quality. This can limit opportunities for the development of local products in the domestic market.

Low local demand for content is a phenomenon where locally created products, services, or works struggle to attract a national audience, often due to a preference for foreign products or a perception of lower quality in local offerings. This situation limits opportunities for local creators and producers to develop their domestic market and thrive.

The causes of weak local demand include:

- Preference for foreign products: Consumers may be attracted by the image of foreign brands, often associated with a certain social prestige or superior quality.
- Perception of inferior quality: There may be a prejudice that local products are of lower quality than international products.
- Stronger marketing for foreign brands: International brands often have larger marketing budgets and more effective strategies, allowing them to dominate the media space and shape consumer preferences.
- Lack of infrastructure: Insufficient investment in infrastructure, transportation, or logistics can hinder the efficient distribution of local products, making them less accessible to consumers.
- Lack of promotion: The local product may suffer from a lack of visibility and appropriate promotion, failing to reach its potential audience.
- Supply chain concerns: Issues with consistency in the quantity and quality of supply can dampen consumer confidence.

To stimulate local demand, it is essential to:

- Improving quality: Investing in training, technology and innovation to improve the quality of local products and services.
- Do targeted marketing: Develop marketing campaigns that highlight the unique advantages of the local product, such as authenticity, culture or local economy.
- Establish strategic partnerships: Collaborate with distributors, online platforms and local media to increase the visibility of the national product.
- Educating the public: Launching awareness campaigns to inform consumers about the benefits of buying local and the quality of national products.
- Developing skills: Investing in training local workers to improve the quality and efficiency of production, making local businesses more competitive.
- The issue of purchasing power and the increase in the household budget: ensuring an adequate wage policy.

The following pages focus on the need to strengthen local capacities

B) Need to strengthen local capacities

It is often necessary to strengthen the capacities of local actors, such as businesses, workers and institutions, to effectively develop and promote local content in Africa.

To achieve this, targeted and multidimensional strategies must be adopted. The following measures can be implemented:

For local businesses

- Mentoring and technical support: establishing mentoring and training programs to help local businesses improve their management, production quality and compliance with international standards.
- Access to financing: facilitating access to credit and investment for small and medium-sized enterprises (SMEs)

to enable them to acquire the equipment and technologies necessary for their development.

- Networking: encouraging the creation of local partnerships and supply chains by connecting local businesses with foreign investors.
- Improving competitiveness: supporting the structural transformation of companies so that they can meet the quality and quantity requirements of local and international markets.

For local workers

- Vocational training: developing vocational and technical training programs aligned with the needs of industries and businesses operating on the continent.
- Partnerships with the private sector: encouraging international companies to partner with local training institutions to transfer skills and technologies.
- Skills development: focus on developing essential skills for social inclusion and participation in the labor market.
- Education: filling educational gaps to improve the overall level of available human capital.

For the institutions

- Institutional and legal support: developing and implementing clear and incentive-based regulatory frameworks for local content development, and ensuring their enforcement.
- Inter-sectoral collaboration: strengthening cooperation between governments, the private sector, civil society organizations and communities to ensure a coordinated and inclusive approach.
- Technology transfer: encouraging the transfer of technology and know-how to local institutions and businesses.

- Promoting a culture of entrepreneurship: fostering an environment conducive to innovation and initiative within communities.
- To ensure social guarantees and quality working conditions.

Conclusion

This chapter addressed the challenges to the effective implementation of local content development policies in Africa. I discussed the lack of technical and technological capacity, inadequate infrastructure, limited access to financing, international competition, a complex regulatory and administrative framework, weak local demand, and the need to strengthen local capacities. I made proposals that I consider appropriate for promoting local content, including internal capacity building through training and workshops, coaching and mentoring, and targeted recruitment of freelancers and new talent. I suggested diversifying financial instruments, improving the business environment, leveraging digital technologies, securing government support, and strengthening cooperation. It is also essential to promote regulatory reforms, streamlined procedures, good governance, strategic partnerships, investment in training and public education, and effective marketing.

By overcoming these challenges, local actors in Africa can promote local content development, stimulate innovation, and create jobs. The next study focuses on the institutional framework and stakeholder roles in the implementation of sectoral and national policies for local content development in the Democratic Republic of Congo.

Chapter III

Institutional framework and roles of stakeholders in the implementation of sectoral and national policies for local content development in the Democratic Republic of Congo

This chapter focuses on the institutional framework and roles of stakeholders in the implementation of sectoral and national policies for local content development in the Democratic Republic of Congo.

It is organized around the following points: local content and the reform of the institutional framework and the roles of stakeholders in the implementation of local content policies.

I. Local content and institutional framework reform

According to the 2023 report from the Central Bank of Congo, 99.6% of exports from the Democratic Republic of Congo (DRC) came from the extractive sector: mining and hydrocarbons. In other words, the country relies heavily on the extractive sector for its development. This lack of economic diversification creates a crippling dependence for the country. Like the DRC, several African countries are counting on mining and hydrocarbons for their development (from Madagascar, through South Africa, Mozambique, Zambia, the DRC, Congo, Gabon, Guinea, Niger, Mali, Nigeria, and others).

Industrial mining in the DRC dates back more than a century, to the creation of the Union Minière du Haut Katanga, the forerunner of Gécamines. After Congo gained its independence, the mining boom reached its peak in the late 1980s. Over the years, mirroring the country's decline, the mining sector collapsed until, in 2002, major reforms were implemented, notably the promulgation of the mining code, which was revised in 2018. This law, enacted after a bitter dispute between some of the heads of major mining companies and the Congolese state, strengthens the DRC's ability and its population to derive greater benefits from mining and thus reduce poverty. Policymakers had concluded that one of the most effective ways to tackle poverty was to involve local populations, directly or indirectly, in mining operations so they could benefit from the economic dividends of mining wealth. But it wasn't just about limiting themselves to the mining sector. The goal was to go beyond this lucrative sector. This is what is known as local content. This concept refers to the priority use of local resources, national skills, and local services. It can also encompass a wide range of approaches, from mandatory targets to more flexible requirements; these are policies that affect multiple sectors of life.

In the Democratic Republic of Congo, a deliberate choice has been made regarding local content policies. This allows development to begin in the mining industry and extend to other sectors. The use of local content is intended to generate change, leading to economic diversification and, ultimately, wealth creation and poverty reduction.

Upon assuming power in January 2019, the Congolese Head of State pledged to work towards reversing the DRC's growing dependence on foreign aid. To achieve this, he chose to revitalize agriculture through a comprehensive reform. A strategy was adopted: the establishment of Special Economic Zones (SEZs), a policy conceived several years prior. The Congolese Head of State also expressed his ambition to create agricultural brigades in the 132 agricultural production centers scattered throughout the country. " *We can overcome poverty, and we will,* " [2]President Félix Tshisekedi declared in 2019. It is a clear fact that too many resource-rich countries (mines and other resources) often suffer from a lack of economic development. Their economic fabric is frequently undiversified, with weak industrial bases, high unemployment rates, and economies vulnerable to commodity cycles. As we will see later, many of these countries are examining investment and mining codes and contracts to aid their development. These countries often rely on local content policies to achieve economic growth. However, it is important to note that local content policies are not a magic bullet. Experience in some countries shows that local content policies can be successful, just as easily as they can fail. The mixed results of some experiences suggest that countries need to invest heavily to do things right. As we have already highlighted, in the Democratic Republic of Congo, one of the sectors on which political leadership has chosen to focus a new policy is agriculture. Clearly, this involves rethinking the economy and embracing the theoretical thinking of François Quesnay. This 18th-century economist based his theory on the idea that a nation's wealth derives primarily from its agricultural sector. For him, " *the wealth produced by agriculture is distributed among the various categories of the nation. This is the famous Economic Table* ."[3] on the distribution of wealth. Far from the Congo and Africa, a Latin American country has long built its "revolution" on agriculture, but a diversified agriculture. This is Cuba. In their book " *Socialism Cuban Style*," Jean Ortiz and Georges Fournial note that " *in Cuba, agricultural growth must now be based on increased yields. We can therefore understand the priority given to this issue by the country's leaders, and the measures they take: incentives for workers paid 'by the finished field,' based on yield, the introduction of various bonuses, and land designated for self-consumption within public agricultural enterprises. The proliferation of so-called 'genetic' farms has made it possible to*

---

[2]Félix Tshisekedi, *State of the Nation Address* , before Parliament convened in Congress, December 13, 2019

[3]André PIETTRE, *Economic History: Facts and Ideas,* Cujas Publishers, Paris 1968, p. 75

build up livestock adapted to the country's conditions and thus achieve significant progress in milk and meat production. This rapid and exemplary genetic transformation of livestock constitutes a remarkable advance, which has become a source of inspiration for many Third World countries."

The Democratic Republic of Congo is clearly inspired by nations that have successfully diversified their economies. Between its mineral wealth and Quesnay's philosophy, the DRC may have found a balance. The country has focused its local content policy on a complete overhaul of the overall economic ecosystem. But beyond agriculture, investment and ingenuity are also directed towards people and their work. Wealth, or its creation, does not rely solely on agriculture, nor solely on natural resources. Echoing Adam Smith, André Piettre writes in his work, * Histoire Économique*, that "...it is neither precious metals nor land, but first and foremost people and their labor, that make the wealth of nations. "[4]

Since 2002, the DRC has been committed to putting the country into a virtuous circle by carrying out reforms aimed at completely changing the country's economic ecosystem.

As we've already mentioned, it was in 2002 that the DRC initiated a process of profound change to its entrepreneurial ecosystem. That year, the country created the National Agency for Investment Promotion (ANAPI). Years later (in 2009), the country truly committed to improving the business climate with the creation, at the political level, of a Steering Committee for the Reform of Public Enterprises (COPIREP). There was also the Democratic Republic of Congo's accession to OHADA in 2012 and the creation of the One-Stop Shop for Business Creation.

In the same vein, President Tshisekedi implemented a specific policy regarding public structures that contribute to economic creation and prosperity. As we have said, this involves investing in "people and their work." Existing structures have been revitalized, and new ones have been created.

---

[4]André PIETTRE, *Op Cit* p 76

Since assuming the presidency, the Congolese Head of State has been resolutely committed to reforms aimed at revitalizing and structuring the entrepreneurial ecosystem. Indeed, Ordinance-Laws No. 22/030 of September 8, 2022, concerning the promotion of entrepreneurship and startups, and No. 22/031 of September 8, 2022, concerning the promotion of crafts, which establish the rules governing the creation, operation, promotion, and development of entrepreneurship, Small and Medium Enterprises (SMEs), startups, and crafts in the Democratic Republic of Congo, have the advantage of being the first legal texts to coherently encompass the entire institutional framework of the entrepreneurial ecosystem. It is also important to emphasize that this legal framework establishes, for the first time, the definition of what constitutes an SME.

This major reform includes the following structures: the National Steering Committee for Entrepreneurship (CNPE), the Guarantee Funds for Entrepreneurship in Congo (FOGEC), the National Agency for the Development of Congolese Entrepreneurship (ANADEC), the Agency for the Promotion of the Middle Classes (APROCM), the Regulatory Authority for Subcontracting in the Private Sector (ARSP).

1. The National Steering Committee for Entrepreneurship (CNPE)

The CNPE, without prejudice to the powers vested in each Ministry and their respective technical services, is an institutional framework for reflection, guidance, impetus and monitoring of the national entrepreneurship policy and program.

The composition and operating procedures of the National Entrepreneurship Council (CNPE) at the national, provincial, and local levels are established, based on a proposal from the Minister responsible for SMEs. The Entrepreneurship Guarantee Funds in Congo (FOGEC) will also be discussed in the following pages.

2. Entrepreneurship Guarantee Fund in Congo (FOGEC)

Access to financing for MSMEs is guaranteed by the Entrepreneurship Guarantee Fund in Congo (FOGEC), a public institution created by Decree No. 20/032 of October 31, 2020, concerning the establishment, organization, and operation of FOGEC. This institution's mission is to:

(i) Guaranteeing access to financing for Congolese startups, MSMEs and artisans;

(ii) To mobilize and collect financial resources at the national and international level, with a view to guaranteeing access for Congolese Startups, Micro, Small and Medium Entrepreneurs and Artisans to financing for their projects by commercial banks and microfinance institutions;

(iii) To make the funds collected available to agencies and organizations approved by the Central Bank of Congo (BCC), as Specialized Financial Institutions, which act in the name and on behalf of FOGEC, for the purpose of:

- Guarantee access for Congolese Startups, Micro, Small and Medium Entrepreneurs and Artisans to financing for their projects by commercial banks, microfinance and mesofinance institutions, in accordance with the policy defined by the Government in this area;
- Develop innovative financing mechanisms for Startups, Micro, Small and Medium Enterprises, in particular through crowdfunding with or without compensation (donation), with or without interest, with equity participation in the companies concerned, or even as a subsidy;
- Developing meso-finance, in particular through the establishment of

concessional lines of credit, guarantee or technical assistance subsidies for the benefit of Startups, Micro, Small and Medium Enterprises;
- Participate in making seed funding and honor loans available to Congolese entrepreneurs in general, mainly women and young people;

(iv) To carry out any other operation that is directly or indirectly related to its corporate purpose.

I haven't forgotten the Congolese National Agency for Entrepreneurship Development (ANADEC)

3. The Congolese National Agency for Entrepreneurship Development (ANADEC)

Access for MSMEs to appropriate training is ensured by the National Agency for the Development of Congolese Entrepreneurship, a public establishment created by Decree No. 21/032 of October 2, 2021 concerning the creation, organization and operation of ANADEC.

In accordance with Framework Law No. 14/004 of February 11, 2014, on National Education and without prejudice to Law No. 18/016 of July 9, 2016, concerning public-private partnerships, the National Agency for the Development of Congolese Entrepreneurship (ANADEC) is authorized to establish all types of partnerships with a view to creating the Higher School of Entrepreneurship in the Democratic Republic of Congo. This public institution raises awareness and supports young people in entrepreneurship. ANADEC aims to create more jobs by accelerating the promotion of entrepreneurship, particularly among young people. ANADEC encourages young people to be creative, take initiative, and develop their professional skills. ANADEC, formerly OPEC, relies on information and theoretical and practical training to educate entrepreneurs on access to financing in order to foster the emergence of the middle class.

There is also the Agency for the Promotion of the Middle Classes (APROCM) to be mentioned.

4. The Agency for the Promotion of the Middle Classes (APROCM)

The promotion of the middle classes is ensured by the Agency for the Promotion of the Middle Classes, a public establishment created by Decree No. 21/003 of October 2, 2021, concerning the creation, organization and operation of APROCEM.

This agency's mission is to conduct studies to promote the emergence of the middle classes; APROCM also works to identify the middle classes and their stratification across the country; APROCM also has the mission of supporting businesses and proposing to the government measures to support and promote the Congolese middle classes.

The lines below refer to the Regulatory Authority for Subcontracting in the Private Sector (ARSP).

5. The Regulatory Authority for Subcontracting in the Private Sector (ARSP)

The regulation of subcontracting activities in the private sector is ensured by the Subcontracting Regulatory Authority in the Private Sector, a public establishment created by Decree No. 19/018 of May 24, 2018, as amended and supplemented by Decree No. 25/20 of October 12, 2020.

This public administrative establishment fulfills a four-part mission: planning, consultation, and control.

In terms of planning, the ARSP is responsible for:

(i) To design, ensure the implementation and monitoring and evaluation of national policy as well as sectoral policies on local content;
(ii) Conclude with private companies in the sector, particularly in mining, hydrocarbons and infrastructure,

specific contracts for the implementation within them of the objectives of sectoral policies on local content and ensure their monitoring.

For consultation purposes:

(i) To design and propose further reforms on the implementing measures of Law No. 17/001 of February 8, 2017 establishing the rules applicable to subcontracting in the private sector and to give an advisory opinion on any measure initiated by the Government in this matter;

(ii) To design and propose to the sectoral Ministers the implementing decrees of Law No. 17/001 of February 8, 2017 establishing the rules applicable to subcontracting in the private sector;

(iii) Assisting private companies in implementing public decisions and their own local content policy within the framework of corporate social responsibility.

Under the heading of Control:

(iv) Ensure compliance with the required conditions in the conclusion of contracts and in the exercise of subcontracting activities;

Apply the appropriate sanctions provided for in the event of a violation of legal, regulatory and

(i) contractual matters relating to subcontracting;

(ii) Apply the administrative sanction of closure of a company provided for in Article 28 paragraph 2 of the Law establishing the rules applicable to subcontracting in the private sector;

(iii) Proceed, in accordance with the conditions set out in Ministerial Decree No. 02/CAB/MIN/CMPMEA/2021 of 06 January 2021 setting out the conditions and procedures for the identification and registration of companies eligible to carry out subcontracting activities in the private sector, in order to establish a database to be used in particular as a basis for calls for tenders and for control carried out by the ARSP;

(iv) Publish the list of eligible subcontractors according to their areas of activity.

This structure is called upon, according to the Local Content Law, to regulate Local Content in the private sector.

It is noted that the regulation of local content in the public sector, in this case, public procurement and public-private partnership, has been entrusted to the Public Procurement Regulatory Authority , ARMP for short, created by Decree.

Indeed, it is clear that the exercise of subcontracting activities in the private sector is conceived as one of the requirements of local content in that it allows companies with majority Congolese capital to access private markets by integrating into the value chains of main companies.

A company with majority Congolese capital is one which, in accordance with Article 3 of Decree No. 18/018 implementing Law 17-001 of February 8, 2017 establishing the rules applicable to subcontracting in the private sector, meets the following criteria:

1. The head office is located in the Democratic Republic of Congo;

2. The majority of the share capital is held by natural or legal persons of Congolese nationality;

3. The management bodies are mostly administered by Congolese individuals;

4. The staff is essentially made up of natural persons of Congolese nationality.

The implementation of local content requirements relating to subcontracting activities in the private sector is carried out in accordance with Law 17-001 of February 8, 2017, which sets out the rules applicable to subcontracting in the private sector.

The essential provision of the law on subcontracting is that subcontracting activity is reserved for companies with majority Congolese capital, managed by Congolese people, regardless of their legal form, whose registered office is located on the national territory.

However, when there is an unavailability or inaccessibility of the expertise mentioned in the paragraph above, and provided that proof is given, in particular by demonstrating to the Regulatory Authority for Subcontracting in the Private Sector the unsuccessful nature of a call for tenders, the main company may, on the basis of the periodic derogation subject to evaluation, granted to it by the said Authority, resort to any other company under Congolese law or to a foreign company during the relevant period.

Outline of some rules relating to local content in the DRC

In the Democratic Republic of Congo, local content development policies have been implemented in certain sectors of economic life without real coherence and appropriate monitoring.

In the mining sector, for example, the country aims to maximize the local benefits of industrialization. In its study entitled " *Innovation of the new mining legislation in the Democratic Republic of Congo: opportunities, challenges and implementation prospects,* " the NGO Natural Resource Governance The institute states that "the employment and training of Congolese people are among the local content elements provided for in the revised mining code (Mining Code 2018) [5]".

Article 405 sexies of the mining regulations in the Democratic Republic of Congo stipulates that *"the holder of mining or quarrying rights, the lessee, and the holders of authorizations as processing or transformation entities shall establish and implement a training program for identified Congolese personnel, covering all qualifications, to enable them to acquire the skills required by the company's management in order to occupy management and supervisory positions within ten years of the start of commercial production* ." A quota is defined by law.

The same requirement applies to employment. Article 405 quinquies of the Mining Regulations stipulates that *"the holder of mining or quarrying rights, the lessee, and the holders of authorizations as a processing or transformation entity must comply with labor legislation regarding employment, in particular the regulations governing the employment of foreigners concerning authorized percentages, those establishing the list of jobs prohibited to foreigners, and the regulations determining the conditions for hiring foreigners. All other things being equal, the holder of mining or quarrying rights, the lessee, and the holders of authorizations as a processing or transformation entity shall give priority to recruiting nationals*. "

---

[5]Natural Resource Governance Institute: Innovation in the new mining legislation in the DRC, July 2019

The table below shows the minimum quota of Congolese employees by category at the different phases of a mining project.

JOB CATEGORY	PROJECT PHASE				
	Research Mining	Development and construction	Commercial production		
			1st - 5th year	6th - 10th grade	11th and beyond
Management executives	20%	25%	60%	65%	70%
Supervisory frameworks	30%	35%	70%	75%	80%
Skilled workers	60%	40%	80%	85%	90%
Maneuvers	80%	85%	90%	95%	100%

With regard, in particular, to the participation of Congolese people in the share capital of mining and/or telecommunications companies operating in the Democratic Republic of Congo, it should be noted that there are legal provisions that can promote the development of local content in these sectors.

Indeed, Article 40 of Law No. 20/017 of November 25, 2020 relating to telecommunications and information and communication technologies stipulates that the legal entity benefiting from a license must be in the form of a Public Limited Company "SA" and that, without prejudice to the agreements and conventions to which the Congolese State is a party, at least thirty percent (30%) of the share capital of the company benefiting from a license in the telecommunications sector is distributed as follows:

(i) At least 25% must be held by Congolese individuals or legal entities whose shares are held by Congolese individuals. This subscription must be effective within three years of the company's incorporation;

(ii) 5% are reserved for Congolese workers of the Company.

In the mining sector, article 71bis of the mining code provides for the participation of natural persons of Congolese nationality in the share capital of mining companies: when the mining company is constituted, the legal obligation is made for the company to have Congolese natural persons participate in its share capital at a rate of at least 10%.

In accordance with Article 144 bis of the Mining Regulations, shares or equity interests reserved for Congolese citizens may be acquired as follows: 5% to one or more Congolese citizens eligible to purchase the shares or equity interests; and 5% to the mining company's employees. Upon application for or transfer of a Small Mining Permit, any foreign national must establish a company under Congolese law in partnership with one or more Congolese citizens, whose participation must be at least 25% of the share capital.

These provisions suffer from ineffective implementation, particularly due to a lack of transparency regarding the origin of local capital resulting from the absence of stock market regulations.

To address this deficiency, the Congolese government intends to establish a stock market as a tool to mobilize domestic and international savings to finance the national economy. According to the DRC Ministry of Finance, as reported by the online news site Agence Ecofin, this mechanism aims to *"provide the country with a legal framework that can facilitate the mobilization of capital for the long-term financing of the national economy."*

“This announced stock market represents an opportunity for Congolese people to become shareholders in local companies and to grow their savings. Congolese companies, for their part, will be able to mobilize longer-term resources to finance their growth and development. The opening of the stock exchange could also strengthen the country's attractiveness to foreign investors," according to the article published by the online site Agence Ecofin.

The Democratic Republic of Congo aims to leverage local content to advance its fight against poverty. Local content is therefore an economic tool used to develop human resources and make better use of natural resources.

Local content is a tool for inclusive development. However, implementing local content policies is not a panacea in itself. It is still necessary to mobilize energy, expertise, and the rigor of the law to fully benefit from local content policies. Political leaders, economic actors, industry leaders, and consumers in general must demonstrate goodwill and a broad commitment to the success of local content policies.

The establishment of the legal framework for local content in the Democratic Republic of Congo

The enactment of the local content law marks a decisive step forward in structuring the Congolese legal framework for national participation in the economy. This law now sets out the requirements applicable to local content in the public and private sectors in the Democratic Republic of Congo, with the aim of fostering the emergence of a strong, competitive, and sustainable national middle class and national champions.

All companies operating within the national territory, regardless of their sector of activity, with the exception of micro-enterprises, Local SMEs, SMIs and startups are subject to requirements relating to the development of local content.

This law applies to all projects financed by public resources or carried out by operators within the framework of so-called public-private partnership contracts.

It also applies to projects undertaken by private sector investors in the Democratic Republic of Congo with the following objectives, in particular:

1. increase added value and job creation for nationals in the value chain through the use of national expertise as well as local goods and services;
2. to promote the participation of Congolese people in businesses across all sectors of the country's economy;
3. to promote the development and availability of a skilled and competitive national workforce;
4. develop national capacities in the value chain through education, training, technology and know-how transfer, as well as research and development;
5. strengthen the competitiveness of Congolese-owned companies by facilitating their access to financing, making compliance with Congolese standards mandatory for products, systems and processes, and promoting certified products on the national and international market;
6. establish a transparent and reliable monitoring and evaluation mechanism for obligations related to Local Content;
7. facilitate the development of the skills of Congolese suppliers by encouraging partnerships with more advanced and experienced foreign companies;
8. to foster the emergence of national champions.

Technically, the law establishes a flexible normative architecture, stipulating that the mandatory guidelines defining the requirements of local content are specified in the National Local Content Plan, a strategic instrument for the implementation and operationalization of its provisions.

On the proposal of the Local Content Regulatory Authority, in synergy with the entire entrepreneurial ecosystem, the Government is developing and implementing a National Local Content Plan with a view to promoting, in particular, local employment, financing, the protection and equitable promotion of women, young people and people living with disabilities, the use of locally produced goods and services, the use of local capital, skills development, technology transfer, environmental protection and the development of local communities.

The following lines emphasize the roles of stakeholders in the implementation of local content policies.

II. Roles of stakeholders in the implementation of local content policies

The success of local content does not depend solely on laws or political intentions. It also relies on a robust institutional ecosystem, in which each actor plays a specific role.

Without effective coordination between institutions, the private sector, local communities and civil society, policies remain theoretical and impacts limited.

This is why we are examining the essential role of each actor, as well as the institutional mechanisms indispensable to ensure coherent, effective and sustainable implementation.

I am talking about the role of the State, the role of specialized agencies in regulation and control, the role of multinational companies, the role of local SMEs as a real driver of local content, the role of universities and research centers, local communities, civil society and the media, the diaspora, inter-institutional coordination as the key to success for the valorization of local content and finally investment for an integrated economy.

I. The role of the State: architect of local content

The State is the initiator, the strategist and the guarantor of local content.

His leadership must be embodied through four essential missions:

1. Define the vision and the legal framework

The State must:

• develop clear and applicable laws;

• set minimum and progressive quotas for local content;

• integrate mandatory clauses into mining, oil, energy and industrial contracts, etc.;

• to ensure regulatory stability.

An unstable or fluctuating policy discourages investors and weakens the local ecosystem.

2. Develop essential infrastructure

Roads, electricity, internet, water, industrial zones: these infrastructures are the physical foundation of local content.

3. Support training and skills development

The State must:

- finance vocational training centers;
- modernize technical universities;
- encourage partnerships between the State, businesses, and universities.

4. Guarantee transparency and fairness

A credible public policy is based on:

- transparent tendering processes;
- regular audits;
- sanctions in case of non-compliance;
- public access to information on contracts.

What can we learn from the role of specialized agencies in regulation and control?

II. The role of specialized agencies: regulation and control

In several countries, and particularly in the DRC, agencies like the ARSP (Regulatory Authority for Subcontracting in the Private Sector) play a pivotal role.

1. Main tasks:
- Certify local businesses;
- Ensure the monitoring and evaluation of local content policies;
- Monitoring the compliance of multinational corporations;
- Encourage the creation of internal value chains;
- Supporting local businesses;
- Publish annual public reports

2. Need for functional autonomy

To be credible, an agency must be:

- independent of political influences;
- endowed with its own budget;
- led by competent and honest professionals;
- equipped with modern verification and certification technologies.

I must acknowledge the role of multinational corporations in the following lines.

III. The role of multinational corporations

The extractive industry and major infrastructure projects are often driven by multinational corporations. These corporations should be partners, not adversaries, in promoting local content.

1. Expected obligations:
- Strict adherence to local employment quotas;
- Use of local suppliers;
- Participation in training programs;
- Technology transfer;
- Contribution to community development;
- Transparent reporting on their local content obligations
2. Advantages for multinational corporations:

- reduction of logistics costs;
- enhanced social acceptability;
- brand image improvement;
- reduction of operational risks;
- operational stability.
- I would like to emphasize in the following point the role of local SMEs as a real driver of local content.

IV. The role of local SMEs: a real driver of local content

SMEs represent the heart of the national economic fabric.

1. Their essential contribution:

- Creation of local jobs
- Production of the goods and services required in the value chain
- Innovation adapted to the local context
- Stabilization of the national economy
- Strengthening the country's resilience

2. The difficulties they face

- limited access to financing;
- lack of skills;
- competition from foreign companies;
- complex administrative procedures;
- lack of quality standards;
- poor visibility.

Local content aims precisely to remove these obstacles.

Universities and research centers have a role to play in the growth of local content.

V. The role of universities and research centers

No sustainable industrial progress is possible without a high-performing education system.

1. Strategic Missions

- Training in technical skills
- Applied research related to the country's needs
- Partnership with companies to develop new technologies
- Establishment of incubators and innovation laboratories
- Skills certification

2. Integration into the value chain

Universities must work hand in hand with:

- the manufacturers,
- public agencies,
- professional communities.

This is the condition for creating a knowledge-based economy.

The role of local communities should not be overlooked.

VI. The role of local communities

They are often the first to be affected by extractive and industrial projects.

1. Priority expectations:

- Jobs for young people
- Development of local infrastructure
- Social programs (schools, hospitals, drinking water)
- Ecological restoration
- Fair compensation

2. Participation in the process

Communities must be:

- consulted;
- associated with the decisions;
- represented in the monitoring committees;

- informed about the rights and obligations of businesses.

It is desirable that civil society and the media get involved in mobilizing for local content.

VII. The role of civil society and the media

They constitute the "eyes and ears" of the public.

1. Key Missions

- Independent monitoring of contracts

- Reporting abuses

- Public awareness

- Promotion of economic patriotism

- Increased transparency

2. Partnerships with public institutions

Civil society must be a strategic partner, not an adversary.

The diaspora remains an untapped resource, as I point out in the following section.

VIII. The role of the diaspora: an untapped resource.

The diaspora represents:

- billions of dollars in capital;
- rare skills;
- international networks;
- valuable technical experience.

1. Strategies for mobilizing the diaspora

- Diaspora sovereign wealth funds

- Dedicated industrial zones

- Tax incentives

- Preferential access to public procurement

- Skills transfer programs

- Occasional technical missions in the DRC

What needs to be clearly understood is that inter-institutional coordination is the key to success in promoting local content.

IX. Interinstitutional coordination: key to success

Effective implementation of local content requires:

- coordination between ministries;
- harmonization between agencies;
- collaboration between provinces;
- ongoing communication with the private sector;
- centralized and digitalized monitoring and evaluation.

Without coordination, each institution moves forward alone, creating a confused and inefficient system.

Investment is needed for an integrated economy.

X. Towards an integrated ecosystem

Local content is not an isolated policy.

It is a system, composed of: laws, institutions, infrastructure, businesses, workers, technologies, and communities. When all these elements work in synergy, the country enters a virtuous cycle of endogenous development.

Conclusion

This chapter focused on the institutional framework and roles of stakeholders in the implementation of sectoral and national policies for local content development in the Democratic Republic of Congo.

The concept of local content refers to the priority use of local resources, national skills, and local services. It encompasses approaches ranging from mandatory objectives to more flexible requirements. It involves policies affecting multiple sectors of life. Development can begin in the mining industry and extend to other areas, including agriculture, investment, and human intelligence and economic activity.

Two points were addressed: local content and the reform of the institutional framework on the one hand, and on the other hand, the roles of stakeholders in the implementation of local content policies. Regarding the first point, I mentioned the Entrepreneurship Guarantee Fund in Congo (FOGEC), the National Agency for the Development of Congolese Entrepreneurship (ANADEC), the Agency for the Promotion of the Middle Classes (APROCM), before discussing the Regulatory Authority for Subcontracting in the Private Sector (ARSP) as the regulator of subcontracting and local content in the private sector. I also pointed out that the regulation of local content in the public sector, in this case, public procurement and public-private partnership, has been entrusted to the Public Procurement Regulatory Authority (ARMP) and the consecration of the legal framework for local content in the Democratic Republic of Congo following the promulgation on June 30 of Law No. 26/018 on local content in the Democratic Republic of Congo. As a second point, I reviewed the role of specialized agencies in regulation and control, that of multinational companies, local SMEs as the real driver of local content, universities and research centers, local communities, civil society and the media, the diaspora, and inter-institutional coordination as the key to success for promoting local content. investing for an integrated economy.

The question that remains open is what strategies should be implemented to promote local content in Africa, using the Democratic Republic of Congo as an example?

Chapter IV

Strategies to promote local content in Africa: the case of the Democratic Republic of Congo

This chapter is based on the strategies to be implemented for the promotion of local content in Africa, using the Democratic Republic of Congo as an example.

Africa is becoming the global demographic center of gravity, shifting from North to South. The Congo, a country of nearly 15 million inhabitants in 1960, is projected to have just over 100 million in 2025. According to UN projections from the World Population Prospects, the African population is expected to more than double by 2100. In 75 years, Africa will have around 3.8 billion inhabitants, compared to 1.5 billion in 2025. This means that the pressure on the job market will continue to grow. Demographic change is an irreversible reality. Young people will be competing for jobs and housing. Hence the need to consider the future of work today for future generations. As we have already touched upon, while the African continent will experience rapid population growth, forecasts for economic progress and overall development will not keep pace with Africa's demographics. In fact, these two trends will be inversely proportional. Forecasts for the development of the African continent are pessimistic. Africa will likely remain prey to recurring crises... write Nicole Gnesotto and Giovanni Grevi [6],

[6] N. GNESOTTO, G. GREVI, The World in 2025, Robert Laffont

who emphasize that in many regions of Africa, " environmental degradation is likely to worsen, particularly due to water scarcity, land overexploitation, and unbalanced urbanization. Despite high fertility rates fueling explosive population growth, life expectancy is likely to remain low due to poverty and inadequate healthcare infrastructure. Most economies will remain dominated by the primary sector, and raw materials will remain the main source of exports to global markets." While some states are likely to experience strong growth, the continent as a whole will continue to decline relative to Asia and South America [7].

These forecasts predict a particularly difficult future for the African continent, which must rely on intelligent policies to avert the more or less dire situation that looms before it. That said, promoting local content in Africa is becoming an economic, cultural, and strategic imperative. It aims to strengthen internal value chains, reduce dependence on imports, and place local expertise, human resources, and businesses at the heart of major economic projects. For this ambition to become a reality, a clear strategy, accompanied by concrete tools, is essential. Regarding the primary sector, several African countries have, over the past decade, reviewed their investment and mining codes and contracts to facilitate development. Beyond mining laws that stipulate the obligation to enforce local content requirements, some countries are going even further by implementing specific local content laws.

Intergovernmental Forum on Mining, Minerals, Metals and Sustainable Development Metals and Sustainable The International Group for Development (IGF), established at the 2002 United Nations World Summit on Sustainable Development in Johannesburg, South Africa, and comprising nearly 87 member countries, states in one of its reports that: *"Over the past decade, a growing number of mining countries*

---

[7]N. GNESOTTO, G. GREVI, *Op. Cit.*

have implemented national strategies to promote industrialization. These strategies include domestic mineral processing and the development of local supply chains. This is due to increasing public pressure, particularly from countries that have not benefited from the mining sector."

This type of industrial strategy often involves measures to retain some raw materials for domestic use. One of the most frequently used instruments is the local content policy. In the mining context, this involves incentivizing or requiring mining companies to process all or part of the extracted materials in the country of origin or to transfer them to others for processing into higher value-added products.

These policies aim to develop the underlying industrial sector and increase the value of exports. They are also fueled by more political motivations, such as growing tensions related to rising youth unemployment, electoral promises made in mining areas, and unresolved colonial or historical legacies.

The development of downstream industries is often seen as a diversification strategy targeting sectors perceived as less sensitive to economic boom-bust cycles. The main objective is to create positive impacts, including outside the mining sector. This leads to the development of value and/or supply chains that broaden the sector's contribution to socioeconomic development, thereby reducing fiscal dependence. Successful diversification can thus generate jobs, be a source of accelerated growth, and increase tax and trade revenues.

The authors of the IGF report ask what lessons can be learned from international experience and conclude that *"international experience shows that the results of this type of strategy are rather mixed. Indeed, few countries have succeeded in their transition through local content policies alone, as these were often developed hastily or based on a political decision aimed at prohibiting the export of unprocessed raw materials without yet having the industrial capacity to process them locally."*

This was the case, for example, with cobalt in 2008 and copper in 2011 in the Katanga province of the Democratic Republic of Congo; with tanzanite in 2007 and mineral concentrates and ores (including gold, copper, nickel, and silver) in 2017 in Tanzania; with chromium in 2011 in Zimbabwe; and with nickel and tin ore in Indonesia in 2014. Some of these measures were quickly abandoned due to a lack of local production capacity or infrastructure, or because they caused unsustainable economic damage. The results of these policies have therefore not been very convincing.

Other countries have been more successful with their local content policies. Botswana has often been cited as having successfully negotiated and secured from De Beers a portion of the sorting and sale of diamonds in the country, which were previously handled in London. Another interesting example, despite its limited oil resources, is Singapore, which has leveraged its world-class infrastructure and logistics networks, particularly its port, to become a major regional hub. The country has successfully attracted oil refineries and other petrochemical industries to its free trade zones, thus becoming a significant regional center for oil trading.

The success or failure of local content policies aimed at boosting the value added of raw materials, and in particular the development of downstream linkages, necessarily depends on good governance of the sector. Government ambitions for the sector must also be aligned with national development plans and policy and regulatory frameworks. Rules governing local content must remain realistic and be designed according to available industrial capacity. They must not become obstacles, as this could jeopardize the development of the industry as a whole.

Simply being rich in natural resources is not enough to guarantee the success of transforming raw materials into finished products. Certain fundamentals are necessary to attract and retain investment in processing industries, including: (i) access to a guaranteed market – national, regional, or international , for the sale of the finished product, as upstream investments in processing activities are often costly; (ii) the existence of efficient and competitive infrastructure, such as transport and communications; (iii) a secure and reliable energy supply; (iv) a skilled and competitive workforce; and (v) a business climate conducive to private sector development, such as measures to facilitate investment, access to credit at competitive rates, and the absence of administrative barriers .

The Democratic Republic of Congo (DRC) stands out for the breadth of its potential, which is natural, human, and cultural. Its vast territory, rich in mineral, forestry, and agricultural resources, offers a solid foundation for sustainable economic development. Furthermore, its youth constitutes a considerable strength: the majority of the population is under 25, representing a dynamic human capital capable of innovating and creating new businesses. Cultural diversity, manifested in local languages, traditions, and expertise, is also an asset for promoting authentically Congolese products and services, capable of finding both national and international markets.

These assets, to give a bit of background, have always existed and already, in the time of the Belgian Congo, they served as the basis for the development policy of the colony in agricultural, mining and manufacturing production hubs according to regional specificities and linked together by roads and railways.

For decades, however, the DRC has been overly dependent on external aid and foreign investment, which has often prioritized the extraction of raw materials for export rather than supporting local processing and national capacity building. This approach has hampered domestic industrial development and limited job creation for the local population, leaving the country vulnerable to fluctuations in international markets and the influence of external partners.

Given this situation, it is imperative to reorient development towards an endogenous approach, where the country's resources and talents are fully mobilized. Local content, whether manufactured goods, innovative services, digital technologies, or cultural creations, must become the driving force behind a self-reliant economy. This requires a coherent strategy aimed at stimulating local businesses, strengthening the skills of young Congolese people, protecting and promoting traditional know-how, and modernizing the infrastructure necessary for the production and distribution of local goods.

The internal development of the DRC can only succeed if all stakeholders in the country – government, businesses, universities, associations, and citizens – commit to a collective approach. The goal is to create a virtuous circle where local production meets the needs of the population, generates income, stimulates innovation, and allows the DRC to position itself as a strong and independent economic player on the continental and global stage. Promoting local content is therefore not merely an economic issue; it constitutes a genuine strategic lever for the country's sovereignty, resilience, and long-term prosperity.

It is necessary to develop the Congolese potential, a national strategy focused on the interior

1. To develop Congolese potential

Harnessing the potential of the Congo is the foundation of any sustainable local content strategy. The Democratic Republic of Congo is a vast country with diverse economic, social, and cultural facets. Each of its regions possesses unique resources that, if better utilized and integrated into a coherent national economy, could transform the country into a true African economic powerhouse. Local content, in this context, is not limited to artisanal or agricultural production; it encompasses all productive activities, from agriculture to industry, culture to technology, energy to services, that originate and develop from the country's internal resources.

Katanga, for example, remains one of the economic powerhouses of the DRC. Its subsoil is rich in strategic minerals such as copper, cobalt, and lithium, essential to the global battery and renewable energy industries. Yet, most of these resources are exported in their raw state, depriving the country of the benefits associated with industrial processing. Developing Katanga's potential therefore means investing in local refining plants, encouraging partnerships between mining companies and technical universities, and creating stable jobs for local youth. It also means making Katanga a center for innovation and mining transformation, capable of competing with the continent's major industrial hubs.

To this end, it is important to create the conditions for the implementation of, in particular, Article 342 ter of the Mining Code, which reads as follows : *"Regarding the time limit for the application of the obligation to process and transform minerals in the Democratic Republic of Congo for current holders of mining rights. Holders of valid mining rights have a period of three years to process and transform the mineral substances they have extracted within the territory of the Democratic Republic of Congo. The period stipulated in the first paragraph of this article may only be reduced or extended by an amendment to this provision by both houses of Parliament."*

This provision shall take effect upon the entry into force of this law.

This measure, which is beneficial for local production, can be accompanied by a realistic moratorium depending on the requirements related to infrastructure development, particularly energy infrastructure.

In the east of the country, particularly in Ituri and North Kivu, agricultural resources are impressive: coffee, cocoa, corn, rice, tropical fruits, palm oil… These products, currently exported or sold raw in local markets, could become the foundation of a genuine Congolese agri-food industry. The challenge lies in creating modern processing units in the provinces, encouraging agricultural cooperatives, and linking production to national commercial channels. Such a policy would guarantee food security, create added value, and reduce dependence on imports of processed foodstuffs.

Kinshasa and Lubumbashi, for their part, embody urban dynamism and the emergence of a new generation of entrepreneurs. These two metropolises are witnessing the birth of tech startups and initiatives in digital technology, communication, logistics, and e-commerce. Urban youth are inventing solutions tailored to local realities every day: transportation apps, mobile payment platforms, agricultural management solutions, and digital educational tools. This abundance of initiatives testifies to a paradigm shift: development can and must stem from Congolese creativity.

Promoting local content means recognizing this diversity of talent and resources, and structuring complete economic value chains, from producer to consumer. It also means building bridges between provinces and cities, between rural production and urban markets, and between tradition and modernity. This approach not only creates jobs and strengthens the national economy, but also restores the pride and confidence of the Congolese people in their own ability to build their future.

In my view, a national strategy centered on the home front is needed, as I explain in the following pages.

2. A national strategy focused on the home front.

The true and sustainable development of the Democratic Republic of Congo can only be achieved if it is based on a national strategy conceived, managed, and implemented from within the country. For too long, economic policies have been dictated by imported models, often ill-suited to the Congolese context, or by external imperatives imposed by international partners. However, a country's economic sovereignty is asserted when it decides for itself on its priorities, methods, and development tools. The DRC must therefore build a national strategy focused on local production, processing, and consumption, drawing on its own strengths.

Such a strategy begins with a clear vision of the national economy, based on leveraging available resources. It is no longer simply a matter of producing for export, but of producing to feed, equip, and serve the Congolese people themselves. This implies rethinking the country's industrial policy in favor of systematic local processing: minerals, agricultural products, timber, textiles, and so on. Every raw material must now undergo national value addition before any export. This approach not only creates jobs but also strengthens economic stability, reduces the trade deficit, and stimulates innovation.

An example of the successful implementation of such a strategy to produce food for the Congolese people was tested in Haut-Katanga and Lualaba with the local production of maize and cement. Indeed, the dependence of these provinces in the former Katanga region of Southern Africa was such that any disruption in the supply chain of these products had immediate repercussions on prices and the daily lives of the population. These two provinces managed to reverse this trend by implementing policies that enabled local maize production, by subsidizing farmers, and cement production, by encouraging the establishment of local cement plants. The emblematic case is that of President Tshisekedi's revitalization of the major agricultural projects of the National Service, which manages the Kanyama Kasese center in Haut- Lomami province and which notably produces a considerable quantity of maize, thus stabilizing the supply of this staple food in a large part of the country and thereby creating food self-sufficiency.

Supporting Congolese entrepreneurship is the first pillar of this strategy. Young entrepreneurs today represent a pool of creativity and dynamism. However, they face numerous obstacles: lack of access to credit, insufficient management training, prohibitive taxation, and competition from imports. It is becoming increasingly urgent to create an environment conducive to their growth. The government must establish appropriate financing mechanisms, such as subsidized loans, guarantee funds, and regional incubators to support project promoters. Furthermore, public procurement must allocate a significant portion to domestic production to stimulate domestic demand and send a strong signal in favor of "Made in Congo."

The second fundamental area is training and skills development. The Congolese education system must be redesigned to meet the real needs of the market. Technical and vocational training, long neglected, must be valued and supported, as it forms the basis of any productive economy. The DRC needs engineers, technicians, skilled craftspeople, coders, and researchers capable of transforming local resources into finished products. Universities and higher education institutions must therefore collaborate with businesses to develop training programs directly linked to sectors with high growth potential.

Finally, a sound national strategy must be based on a protective regulatory framework. The Congolese economy can only grow if local businesses are protected from unfair competition from low-priced imported goods. The government must implement intelligent tariff policies that favor domestic production without closing the country off to international trade. This involves establishing quality standards, local certifications, and control mechanisms that enhance the value of Congolese products in their own market. In other words, industrial policy must prioritize the national interest by encouraging domestic investment, local processing, and pride in national products.

For this strategy to succeed, it must be designed and led by the Congolese themselves, based on a principle of national ownership. It is by focusing on the country's priorities and mobilizing its internal potential that the DRC will be able to build a resilient, self-reliant, and inclusive economic model.

The goal here is to define a clear, shared, and measurable vision of local content. Without a national vision, efforts remain scattered and ineffective.

A vision driven by political leadership

Local content must be a presidential and governmental project, that is to say a national priority, explicitly included in: national development plans; industrial policies; sectoral strategies (mining, hydrocarbons, agriculture, digital, energy, etc.); national budgets.

A national consensus

Success also depends on alignment between: the State; public and private companies; civil society; universities and research centers; local authorities.

Local content imposed without social and economic consensus will fail sooner or later.

This vision must be based on internal ownership. The DRC must internalize two fundamental ideas:

- Create wealth within before seeking it outside.
- Local transformation is not an option: it is a necessity.

Having identified the challenges, the issues, the institutional framework and the role of stakeholders, concrete, directly applicable strategies to make local content a true engine of economic transformation in the Democratic Republic of Congo (DRC) must combine political vision, economic measures, technological innovations and strengthening of human capital.

I propose to build a robust, coherent and evolving legal framework, and to develop a national system for certifying local businesses.

I. Consolidate a robust, coherent and evolving legal framework

Following the promulgation of Law No. 26/018 of June 30, 2026 on local content, the challenge now lies in its operationalization through the adoption of implementing regulatory measures, its articulation with existing sectoral legislation and the establishment of a national certification system for local businesses.

1.1. Harmonisation of the legal framework for local content

The Democratic Republic of Congo now has a framework law on local content, intended to be applied across all economic sectors. However, its effectiveness will depend on the Local Content Regulatory Authority, which, depending on the sector, ensures its harmonization with existing sectoral legislation, particularly that relating to mining, hydrocarbons, subcontracting, telecommunications, electricity, and other strategic sectors.

This harmonization aims to prevent regulatory contradictions, overlapping jurisdictions, and areas of legal uncertainty that could weaken the implementation of the national local content policy. It will be ensured through the adoption of regulatory measures stipulated by law, particularly the National Local Content Plan , which will establish strategic guidelines, progressive quotas, monitoring mechanisms, and the obligations applicable to companies subject to it.

1.2. Setting progressive quotas

One of the main instruments for implementing the national local content policy lies in defining progressive, realistic, and differentiated thresholds according to business sectors. In accordance with the Local Content Law, these quotas must be as set out in the National Local Content Plan. This should take into account the actual capacities of the national economic fabric, the requirements of competitiveness, and the objective of a gradual increase in the role of Congolese companies in value chains. To this end, the following proposals could usefully guide the development of this Plan.

I propose the introduction of mandatory clauses in all contracts

1.3. Introduction of mandatory clauses in all contracts

Every contract signed by the State or public companies must contain:

- quantified requirements;
- penalties for non-compliance;
- a plan to contribute to local content.

The pages below propose developing a national certification system for local businesses.

II. Develop a national system for certifying local businesses

The success of local content depends on the ability to identify genuine Congolese businesses. I propose the creation of a national register of local suppliers, with mandatory certification.

2.1. Creation of a National Register of Local Suppliers

This register must be:

- digitized;

• accessible to investors;

• updated in real time;

• Secure to prevent fictitious companies.

I also propose mandatory certification.

2.2. Mandatory Certification

The certification will verify:

• local shareholding;

• governance;

• the actual participation of the Congolese;

• technical capacity.

It seems important to consider setting up "industrial clusters" in the provinces.

III. Establishment of "industrial clusters" in the provinces

The clusters include:

• industries;

• training centers;

• suppliers;

• research centers.

They reinforce regional specialization.

Examples of clusters to be developed in the DRC

• Lualaba / Haut-Katanga: batteries, metallurgy, refining.

• Ecuador: agro-industry, palm oil, processed wood.

• Grand Kasai: processing of maize, cassava, textiles.

• Kongo-Central: logistics, cement, port industries.

• Ituri / North Kivu: coffee, cocoa, horticultural products.

I believe it is essential to develop a funding system dedicated to local content.

IV. Develop a financing system dedicated to local content.

Lack of capital is one of the main obstacles to the growth of small and medium-sized enterprises. The creation of a The Special Fund for the Promotion of Local Content (FNPCL), established by the Local Content Law, is one effective solution to this obstacle. The use of innovative financial instruments should also be considered.

4.1. Special Fund for the Promotion of Local Content (FNPCL)
Placed under the authority of the Minister responsible for Local Content, this fund is intended to finance the capital development of Congolese people, training, research and development, as well as the creation of national champions.

Specifically, I propose that this Fund be used to:

- Granting appropriate financing (equity or strategic loans) enabling nationals with shares in companies with large markets or large industrial, infrastructure and construction projects or others requiring large financing and sometimes requiring state guarantees;

- Guaranteeing the participation of nationals in capital in strategic sectors (mining, energy, construction, telecommunications, agriculture, logistics, industry, etc.);

- Provide funding to nationals to set up military industries to manufacture equipment, security materials and military uniforms;

- Facilitating national investment in strategic banking sectors sectors as part of the promotion of investment banks as provided for by the Local Content Law.

We need innovative financial instruments are also needed.

4.2. Innovative financial instruments

• state guarantees;

• concessional lines of credit;

• development obligations;

• diaspora funding;

• Congolese venture capital.

A national training and skills transfer program is needed.

V. National Training and Skills Transfer Programme

Local content cannot succeed without a human capital revolution.

I propose the "One Million Technical Skills" program, sectoral centers of excellence, and an obligation for multinationals to invest in training.

5.1. “One Million Technical Skills” Programme

Objective: to train 1,000,000 young people in:

• welding,

• industrial electricity,

• geology,

• IT,

• mechanics,

• Industrial maintenance,

• logistics,

• mining restoration.

I propose sector-specific centers of excellence.

5.2. Sectoral Centres of Excellence

One center per sector:

• mines;

• hydrocarbons;

• agriculture;

• energy ;

• digital;

• Construction and Public Works.

Multinational companies need to be required to invest in training.

5.3. Obligation for multinationals to invest in training

Each foreign company will sign a Local Skills Development Plan (PDCL).

What can be said about the national innovation and technology policy?

VI. National Innovation and Technology Policy

I propose the creation of provincial technology parks, incubators for start-ups and the promotion of digital Made in Congo.

6.1. Creation of provincial science parks

Each technology park will be specialized in: AI, blockchain, digital agriculture, cybersecurity, fintech.

There are also incubators for start-ups worth mentioning.

6.2. Start-up incubators

The state must support incubators that help young entrepreneurs develop:

- industrial solutions;
- automation tools;
- management software;
- payment platforms.

It is important to promote digital "Made in Congo" products.

6.3. Promotion of digital Made in Congo

Create an official certification for locally developed technological solutions.

What about the emergence of a national culture of buying local?

VII. Emergence of a national culture of buying local

Local content needs to become a habit, not just an obligation.

7.1. National awareness campaigns " Buy Congo, Build Congo" "Our resources, our wealth" "Congo produces, Congo consumes"

7.2. Integration into schools

Education in economic patriotism.

7.3. Strengthening provincial economic fairs to promote local businesses.

It is important to consider strengthening transparency and governance.

VIII. Strengthening transparency and governance

Without transparency, there can be neither trust nor investment. I propose the complete digitalization of procedures, including a national platform for monitoring local content.

8.1. Complete digitalization of procedures

- awarding of contracts;
- quota control;
- Contract monitoring;
- publication of reports;
- Payment traceability.

A national platform for monitoring local content is needed.

8.2. National platform for monitoring local content

This platform will publish:

- certified companies;
- the compliance rates of multinational companies;
- statistics by province;
- the sanctions applied.

It is important to consider the regular evaluation and adaptation of public policies.

IX. Regular evaluation and adaptation of public policies

Local content must evolve accordingly:

- results;
- national capacities;
- of the global economic situation;

• industrial needs.

A public report must be published annually.

My ultimate vision is to transform the DRC into an African industrial hub.

X. Final vision: to transform the DRC into an African industrial hub

Local content is not an end in itself. It is a strategy for economic sovereignty.

The DRC can become:

• the African capital of electric batteries;

• a regional agro-industrial hub;

• a cultural and digital leader;

• a major energy player;

• an exporter of high value-added finished products.

The proposals outlined above are not intended to be exhaustive or mandatory. They constitute technical and strategic guidelines designed to inform the deliberations of public authorities in developing the implementing instruments for Law No. 26/018 of June 30, 2026, on local content. As such, they may be taken into account, *mutatis mutandis* , during the development of the National Local Content Plan , adapting them to the specific characteristics of each sector of activity, the capacities of the national economic fabric, and the development objectives pursued by the national local content policy.

Conclusion

This chapter focuses on the strategies to be implemented for the promotion of local content in Africa, using the Democratic Republic of Congo as an example.

Faced with the growing population boom in Africa, however with pessimistic forecasts for its development, with major challenges regarding youth, work and housing, the promotion of local resources remains an opportunity as well as an economic, cultural and strategic imperative for the future of the continent.

In the mining context, there is talk of forcing mining industries to transform all or part of the materials extracted in the country for the development of the industrial sector and the increase in the value of exports, to combat tensions related to youth unemployment and electoral promises.

The success of local development depends on good governance, with government ambitions aligned with national development plans and political and regulatory frameworks.

Local content – manufactured goods, innovative services, digital technologies, or cultural creations – must become the driving force behind a self-reliant economy. Promoting local content is therefore not merely an economic issue; it is a true strategic lever for the country's sovereignty, resilience, and long-term prosperity. A national strategy focused on domestic development is essential. I propose three key areas, with support for Congolese entrepreneurship as the first pillar of this strategy. It's crucial to understand that young entrepreneurs today represent a pool of creativity and dynamism. The second area is training and skills development for local communities. A protective regulatory framework is necessary. This requires a vision championed by political leadership and a national consensus among the State, public and private enterprises, civil society, universities, research centers, and local authorities.

It is imperative to make local content a true driver of economic transformation in the Democratic Republic of Congo (DRC). Therefore, it is essential to combine political vision, economic measures, technological innovations, and human capital development. I propose consolidating a legal framework through the harmonization of sectoral laws , creating a National Register of Local Suppliers, establishing industrial clusters in the provinces, creating a financing system dedicated to local content, including the National Fund for the Promotion of Local Content (FNPCL) as stipulated in the Local Content Law, and developing innovative financial instruments, as well as a national training and skills transfer program. A national innovation and technology policy is needed, including the creation of provincial technology parks, startup incubators, and the promotion of digital "Made in Congo." It is crucial to promote a national culture of buying local through national awareness campaigns such as " Buy Congo, Build Congo," "Our Resources, Our Wealth," and "Congo Produces, Congo Consumes." This implies transparency and good governance. Regular evaluation is essential.

During the development of the National Local Content Plan provided for by the Local Content Act, the public authorities shall use the proposals formulated in this chapter as elements that may enrich the debate.

It is now necessary to consider the mandatory principles and guidelines for the implementation of sectoral policies and national policies for local content development in the Democratic Republic of Congo.

Chapter V

Principles and mandatory guidelines for the implementation of sectoral and national policies for local content development in the Democratic Republic of Congo

This chapter focuses on the mandatory principles and guidelines for the implementation of sectoral and national policies for local content development in the Democratic Republic of Congo.

In the following lines, drawing on examples from other African countries, we will first examine, with concrete cases, each principle provided for by the Local Content Law indicated below and, secondly, what the mandatory guidelines of the national local content plan may be.

I. Principles to be respected in the implementation of local content policies

Achieving local content objectives should be based on adherence to the following principles:

1. optimization and protection of the business climate ;
2. strengthening of the national private sector;
3. transparency, fairness and non-discrimination in the implementation of obligations related to Local Content;

4. building of local content implementation institutions;
5. cooperation between stakeholders;
6. promotion of women and youth and protection of people living with disabilities;
7. environmental protection and promotion of sustainable development;
8. responsibility and protection of local communities;
9. setting of local content thresholds by regulatory means, except where legally permitted;
10. promotion of innovation and technology transfer.

- optimization and protecting the business climate

Protecting the business climate in our country is crucial for developing local content. Indeed, a healthy business environment fosters local industry, employment, and innovation. To achieve this, reforms are necessary to improve competitiveness, combat informality, ensure the fair allocation of public contracts, and reduce bureaucracy, thereby enabling Congolese businesses to thrive in the face of imported products and companies benefiting from tax advantages.

Several mechanisms for protecting the business climate can be put in place to address persistent challenges, including: - Cumbersome administrative procedures and corruption, which are major obstacles to improving the business climate; - Weak infrastructure, which hinders economic development and business competitiveness; - An underdeveloped financial sector, making it difficult for local ~~SMEs to access credit and financial services~~ ; - A lack of skilled and well-trained labor, which limits productivity and innovation, forcing companies to recruit abroad; - A lack of QHSE standards: Many local companies do not comply with or are unaware of Quality, Health, Safety and Environment (QHSE) standards, making them less competitive.

The government has pledged to reform the regulatory framework and digitize services to simplify administrative procedures, such as the one-stop shop for business creation.

Tax and customs incentives are offered, particularly in priority sectors and special economic zones.

Efforts are being made to strengthen economic governance through transparency and the digitalization of services. This also includes the establishment of dialogue platforms aimed at improving the business climate through consultation between the public and private sectors.

The legal framework must also be modernized, notably with the establishment of an international arbitration center offering a reliable mechanism for resolving commercial disputes. Furthermore, the domestic private sector must be strengthened.

- Strengthening the national private sector

Strengthening the domestic private sector through local content involves policies that require companies, particularly multinationals, to use goods, services, and labor from the host country in their operations. This stimulates the domestic economy, creates skilled jobs, develops local capacity (such as through technology transfer), and ensures that investments benefit the host country more. Measures such as local procurement requirements, partnerships, and investments in training are commonly used to achieve this, although they must be realistically designed so as not to hinder industrial development, as illustrated by the example of Mali and its mining industry.

Key mechanisms for local content

Supply requirements: Require companies to source goods and services from local suppliers.

Employment and training: Employ local labor and invest in training to improve skills and know-how within the population.

Partnerships: Promote partnerships between foreign and national companies for the transfer of technology and skills.

Adding value: Encourage the addition of value to raw materials at the national level before their export, rather than simply exporting raw materials.

Application examples

Mining industry: Countries like Mali have put in place laws to ensure that the mining sector benefits the country more by strengthening the capacities of Malian companies and promoting local employment.

Oil sector: West African countries such as Ghana, Senegal, Ivory Coast and Nigeria have adopted similar laws to require foreign companies to integrate local businesses and skills into their operations.

Challenges and considerations

Local capabilities: It is essential that local content requirements are realistic and based on available industrial capabilities so as not to become an obstacle to development.

Funding: Lack of funding can be a major obstacle for local businesses, sometimes requiring the implementation of financial support mechanisms.

Taxation and Contract Enforcement: Governments must ensure that contracts are respected and implement systems for fair taxation, thereby preventing revenue losses due to tax evasion or undeclared activity. Transparency is essential for economic growth and the promotion of local content.

- Transparency

Transparency in local content development involves making public information about the implementation of policies aimed at increasing local added value. It fosters trust and accountability by clearly communicating about processes, objectives, local employment, the sourcing of local goods and services, and the participation of local businesses.

Transparency helps to ensure that the objectives of these policies are actually achieved and to verify that economic actors respect their commitments.

Transparency is important because it allows citizens, local businesses, and civil society actors to verify that local content policies are being implemented correctly and are genuinely benefiting the country's economy. It makes procurement and contract awarding processes transparent, reduces the risks of corruption and favoritism, and improves implementation through open communication about processes, decisions, and even challenges encountered. It ensures fair competition between local suppliers and foreign companies, and guarantees that qualified local businesses have a chance to win contracts.

By disclosing information on objectives, results and challenges, transparency encourages accountability from all stakeholders, including businesses and government.

The development of local content can be made more transparent by:

(v) Publication of policies and data: Make public local content policies, local content thresholds required in contracts (e.g., percentage of local sourcing or local employment), and results achieved.

(vi) The creation of simple and accessible databases containing information on local employment versus employment of foreign nationals, on local supply of goods and services, and on the percentage of production processed in the country.

(vii) The publication of regular reports on local content, such as those from the EITI, which describe the implementation of policies and provide quantitative data on the performance of companies.

(viii) The establishment of monitoring and reporting mechanisms, with the support of civil society, to monitor the application of laws and commitments related to local content.

(ix) Clear and honest communication about successes but also about challenges in order to build a culture of trust and collaboration between the stakeholders involved.

Strengthening the capacities of local content implementation institutions is essential, as I argue in the following lines.

- Strengthening the capacities of local content implementation institutions

Strengthening the capacity of local content implementation institutions improves their ability to achieve local content objectives, focusing on skills development, training, access to financial and technical resources, and improving governance processes and mechanisms.

This involves equipping these institutions with the necessary resources to enforce local content laws, monitor progress, and integrate economic and social development aspects, such as job creation and the growth of local businesses. The ultimate goal is to ensure that the exploitation of natural resources generates sustainable local added value and that local businesses and citizens fully benefit from the sector.

Training for managers in public institutions enables them to master the principles of local content and acquire the skills necessary to fully perform their role.

This capacity building also improves processes and governance by establishing robust monitoring and implementation mechanisms, with clear benchmarks and accountability mechanisms for all stakeholders: major companies, public and private institutions. It also ensures that local content policies align with national priorities, such as job creation, skills development, and increased procurement of local goods and services; and that, moreover, the policies are realistic in relation to existing industrial capacities and adapted to sectoral contexts, such as the integration of new technologies. Mutual cooperation among stakeholders is essential.

- Mutual cooperation between stakeholders

Mutual cooperation among stakeholders is essential for the success of local content policies and relies on transparent communication, active engagement, and shared responsibility. It requires that governments, local and international businesses, communities, NGOs, and other actors ensure that policies are aligned with national objectives, create sustainable local economic benefits, and are effectively monitored and enforced.

Each stakeholder must play their part in achieving the set objectives. For governments, this includes, in particular, developing clear local content policies aligned with national priorities, and implementing monitoring and enforcement mechanisms to ensure that companies comply with the objectives.

For businesses (local and international), it will be a matter of actively engaging in local initiatives, reporting on their performance and sharing data to allow for effective evaluation, investing in local capacity building, employment and local procurement.

And finally, for local communities and Non-Governmental Organizations, to participate in dialogue and consultation processes, to help monitor the impact of policies at the community level, and to defend their interests and ensure that policies meet their needs.

It is imperative to support the promotion of women and youth and the protection of people living with disabilities.

- The promotion of women and youth and the protection of people living with disabilities

Policies for developing local content must take into account the promotion of women and youth as well as the protection of people living with disabilities.

What are the key steps and mandatory guidelines for local content development?

II. The essential steps and mandatory guidelines for local content development

I discuss the essential steps in developing local content policies

1. The essential steps in developing local content policies

Several steps are essential in the implementation of local content policies. When these steps are scrupulously followed, they allow for the design and implementation of coherent policies that take into account the specific realities of each country.

These steps are: ensuring compatibility with national development objectives, reviewing the current situation, developing local content policies and monitoring, reviewing and implementing them.

Step 1: Ensure compatibility with the objectives of national development

In developing local content policies in a sector, the DRC must define the role that the sector plays in its national and strategic development plan (PNSD).

A National Development Plan is a strategic document that establishes a country's priorities for achieving its economic growth and development objectives over several years. It defines the public policies and strategies to be followed in key areas such as agriculture, industry, governance, and social development, in order to improve the quality of life for citizens.

In the dedication to the National and Strategic Development Plan of the DRC for the period 2024-2028, President FELIX-ANTOINE TSHISEKEDI clearly indicates that the NSDP constitutes the sole unifying programmatic framework of reference for all interventions by the Government and its development partners during the period from 2024 to 2028.

It is primarily dedicated to the entire population of the Democratic Republic of Congo (DRC) for the trust they placed in him, successively in 2018 and 2023, by willingly accepting to bring him to the top of the State.

Indeed, in order to establish a modern state, to overcome poverty, declared a great national cause to build a strong Congo focused on its development in peace and security, a Congo reconciled with itself, six commitments formed the basis of his election, thus constituting a major political turning point for the process of finalizing the second generation National Strategic Development Plan (PNSD).

This is:

(i) Create more jobs to absorb the tens of thousands of young people who enter the job market each year and reduce the level of underemployment;

(ii) Protect and strengthen the purchasing power of Congolese households;

(iii) Better protect Congolese citizens so that the DRC can move closer to its peaceful vocation for the benefit of the entire Central African and Great Lakes region;

(iv) Ensure greater access to basic services;

(v) To build a more diversified and competitive economy; and

(vi) Strengthen the efficiency of public services.

Furthermore, the country aims to achieve its emerging economy status within 25 years. To do so, numerous conditions must be met to enable it to seize new economic opportunities that can facilitate structural transformation and thus improve the well-being of the population. With this in mind, the National Development Plan (NSDP) has recommended a series of reforms for emerging economy status, focusing on five key areas:

(i) Improving Governance;

(ii) The development of human capital;

(iii) Economic diversification;

(iv) Infrastructure development and land-use planning; and

(v) The sustainable and balanced development of the provinces.

The objective of the entire population, through civil society organizations, youth platforms and the private sector, is therefore to support in a participatory manner the country's progress towards achieving the set development objectives, which are based on the Sustainable Development Goals (SDGs).

Local content policies in a given sector must be part of the overall approach to ensure that investments in that sector play their full potential role in achieving the objectives set by the National

Sustainable Development Plan (NSDP). An assessment of the current situation is necessary.

Step 2: Take stock of the current situation

After defining the objectives, it is important, sector by sector, to study the political, socioeconomic, and other contexts in which investors and sector companies operate. This involves understanding the opportunities and assessing the gaps by considering what types of skills, goods and services, and infrastructure sector companies will need.

Policies for developing local content therefore require that serious studies be carried out in the sectors concerned before they are developed.

It is important to think about the development of local content policies

STEP 3: Developing local content policies

This step refers to the actual determination of mandatory guidelines as well as incentive and support mechanisms.

Monitoring, review, and enforcement are necessary.

Step 4: Monitoring, review and enforcement

Once designed, local content policies must be administered and enforced, and progress must be measured against explicit benchmarks in the form of plans or targets. They must therefore include an integrated, independent monitoring and enforcement mechanism, ensuring that the various stakeholders (including public institutions) are held accountable.

Such a mechanism requires common reporting requirements for private sector companies and robust systems for collecting data on the outcomes of interventions. The mechanism should include a review function, so that failure is not simply punished, but also involves consultation and critical evaluation of the policies themselves with a view to potential revision and improvement. It should also be designed to propose the phase-out of certain support measures when industries become sufficiently competitive to be self-sustaining or if, after a certain period, it is clear that the support measures will not have the desired effects. What, in my opinion, are the mandatory guidelines for local content development?

2. Mandatory guidelines for local content development

Some mandatory guidelines are outlined below for illustrative purposes. The policies related to these guidelines must be implemented in accordance with the steps mentioned above for reasons of efficiency and consistency. These guidelines concern policies related to procurement, direct employment, and local capital.

a) Local sourcing

Policies of this type aim to increase the quantity of locally sourced goods and services purchased by major companies. They are likely to significantly increase the contribution of private sector industry to national GDP. Indeed, they generally have much greater potential than taxes and royalties. Local procurement can eventually serve as a gateway to economic diversification, with suppliers becoming exporters and moving horizontally from extractive sectors to other sectors.

There are three main approaches to implementing local content development policies related to local sourcing, linked to the definition of the term "local".

(i) The geographic approach: "Local" can refer to business activities registered, incorporated or carried out within one of the various geographic boundaries - national, regional, state or provincial, or in communities near the site of the main business;

(ii) The Value Added approach: "Local" can mean that a substantial amount of value has been added within the country. Unlike the geographical definition, this means that goods cannot simply be imported and resold by locals. However, measuring local value added can be difficult;

(iii) Ownership: Local ownership emphasizes participation, which may involve a portion of the local population in management, either as equity owners or as employees. This requirement can be easily circumvented.

There is a wide variety of policies aimed at encouraging local purchasing. On the demand side, these policies focus on creating demand for locally sourced goods and services. They can range from mandatory quotas to voluntary incentives to meet targets. On the supply side, the emphasis is on building the capacity of local suppliers to meet global standards for price, quality, and reliability. Both types of policies are generally necessary. Supplier development helps ensure that demand-side policies do not require more than local businesses can provide. Direct local employment should be promoted.

b) Direct local employment

Local content development policies can aim to create both qualitative and quantitative local jobs through major companies. These policies can be binding and rely on strong compliance mechanisms. They may include, on the one hand:

(i) Percentages of local employment imposed, often different for different types of jobs;

(ii) Requirements to provide training for the local population or to support training facilities;

(iii) Mandatory succession or relocation plans;

(iv) Visa restrictions for foreign workers;

(v) The forced hiring of indigenous populations, women, or disadvantaged groups.

Alternatively, facilitation approaches, which generally rely on incentive policies, offer support and incentives for the development and hiring of local workers such as:

(i) Preferences for the allocation of mining contracts;
(ii) Non-binding requirements to hire local people (e.g., "where possible");
(iii) Tax incentives for hiring locally.

Governments are the only entities capable of influencing both the supply and demand for local employment in a given sector. A government can implement regulations requiring businesses to meet local content requirements; it can also facilitate education and training to prepare the local workforce to meet those requirements. In almost all cases, both types of measures are essential; mere regulation with cover policies, without parallel efforts to ensure the availability of the right skills, is not a recipe for success. And what about local capital?

c) Local capital

In the DRC, as mentioned above, some sectors already require Congolese participation in share capital. These include the mining and telecommunications sectors.

This mandatory participation of nationals in the share capital of each company operating in the private sector has just been extended to all other sectors of the national economy by the Local Content Law in the sense that it stipulates: "subject to provisions under certain applicable sectoral legislation require that any company operating in the private sector, taking into account the transparency rules established in particular for stock markets, guarantee a minimum effective participation of Congolese individuals in its share capital.

In this respect, natural persons of Congolese nationality hold a minimum stake determined according to the sectors of activity and in the same spirit, a minimum stake of 5% is granted to Congolese workers in the following manner:

1. Industry sector:

In Hydrocarbons (oil and gas)

- 8% of shares for individuals
- 5% of shares for workers

Manufacturing industries:

- 20% of shares for natural persons
- 5% of shares for workers

Food and beverage industry:

- 25% of the shares for individuals
- 5% of shares for workers

Textile, clothing and leather industry

- 20% of the shares for individuals
- 5% of shares for workers

Wood, paper, cardboard and printing industry:

- 20% of shares for individuals
- 5% of shares for workers

Chemical and pharmaceutical industry (soaps and detergents, fertilizers, paints and medicines...):

- 20% of shares for individuals
- 5% of shares for workers

Rubber and plastics industry:

- 20% of shares for individuals
- 5% of shares for workers

Metallurgy and metal products industry:

- 20% of shares for individuals
- 5% of shares for workers

Machinery and equipment manufacturing industry:

- 20% of shares for individuals
- 5% of shares for workers;

Automotive industry and transport equipment:

- 20% of shares for individuals
- 5% of shares for workers;

Electronics, IT and optics industry:

- 20% of shares for individuals
- 5% of shares for workers

Furniture and miscellaneous object manufacturing industry (games, toys, jewelry):

- 26% of shares for individuals
- 5% of shares for workers

Tobacco and tobacco-based product manufacturing industry:

- 26% of shares for individuals
- 5% of shares for workers

Electrical, electronic and household appliance manufacturing industry:

- 25% of shares for individuals
- 5% of shares for workers

Energy industry (production, transformation, transport and distribution of energy: electricity, renewables…):

- 26% of shares for individuals
- 5% of shares for workers

Cement industry:

- 25% of shares for individuals
- 5% of shares for workers

Construction materials manufacturing industry (bricks, tiles, lime, glass, plaster, mortar, concrete, reinforcement, insulation, coatings, steel, iron, gravel, rubble, sand, roofing, sheet metal…

- 26% of shares for individuals
- 5% of shares for workers

Craft industries (metalwork, arts and crafts, etc.)

- 30% of shares for individuals
- 5% of shares for workers.

2. Agricultural sector

- 30% of shares for individuals
- 5% of shares for workers.

3. Transport and logistics sector

Air transport: 20% share for individuals

Land transport: 25% share for physical transport.

Maritime transport: 25 shares for natural persons

4. Infrastructure and construction sector (roads, ports, airports, airport terminals)

- 20% of shares for individuals

5. Water sector
   - 26% of shares for individuals
   - 5% of shares for workers.
6. Tourism and HORECA sector
   - 26% of shares for individuals
   - 5% of shares for workers.
7. Forestry, Fishing and Livestock Sector
   - 51% of shares for individuals
   - 5% of shares for workers.
8. Health sector
   - 20% of shares for individuals
   - 5% of shares for workers.
9. Media, Advertising and Marketing Sector
   - 51% of shares for individuals
   - 5% of shares for workers.
10. Trade sector
    - 25% of shares for individuals
    - 5% of shares for workers.
11. Small business sector (wholesale and retail)

100% of shares for natural persons.

It is also important that in public procurement and public-private partnerships (PPPs), quotas are reserved for nationals in the execution of key activities, particularly in the areas of road concessions, construction and rehabilitation of dams and other infrastructure.

.

Conclusion

The fifth chapter focused on the mandatory principles and guidelines for implementing sectoral and national policies on local content development in the Democratic Republic of Congo. I discussed the essential steps in developing local content policies and the mandatory guidelines for local content development.

Among the steps, I recalled the need to ensure compatibility with national development objectives, to take stock of the current situation, the development of local content policies and monitoring, review and application.

Among the principles to be respected in the implementation of local content policies, I propose the protection of the business climate, the strengthening of the national private sector, transparency, the strengthening of the capacities of local content implementation institutions, mutual cooperation between stakeholders and the promotion of women, youth and the protection of people living with disabilities.

As key mechanisms for local content, I propose sourcing requirements that obligate companies to purchase goods or services from local suppliers; employment and investment in staff training to improve skills and know-how; partnerships between foreign and domestic companies for technology and skills transfer; and value addition to raw materials at the national level before export. I support mandatory guidelines for local content development. These guidelines address policies related to sourcing, direct employment, and local capital.

The development of local content should no longer be confined to secondary activities, such as subcontracting. As mentioned above, the State must fill the existing legal void by establishing a stock market that allows nationals to become shareholders in major companies, either individually or collectively, in a fully transparent manner. The tools for developing local content should now be considered in the final chapter.

Chapter VI

Tools for developing local content

The final chapter focuses on tools for developing local content.

No matter how ambitious a strategy, it cannot be effective without concrete tools for its implementation. Promoting local content in the DRC must be based on a coherent set of economic, financial, institutional, and technological tools capable of supporting private initiative, stimulating production, and ensuring the competitiveness of Congolese products on the national and African markets.

The first essential tool lies in financial instruments. It is necessary to create an environment where Congolese entrepreneurs, artisans, farmers, and innovators can access financing on favorable terms. The State, through the Development Bank of Congo and partner institutions, should establish SME support funds, low-interest loans for local projects, and targeted subsidies to encourage applied research and technical training. Large mining and oil companies operating in the DRC could also be required to finance programs supporting local production, as part of their corporate social responsibility.

The second tool concerns strategic partnerships. Developing local content cannot be the sole responsibility of the government. It requires the coordinated mobilization of the state, the private sector, and academia. These partnerships should strengthen scientific research, modernize production tools, and open markets for Congolese products. For example, collaboration between universities and mining industries can foster the creation of new local extraction and processing technologies. Similarly, alliances between provinces and local businesses can enable the development of regional resources within a framework of balanced development.

The third tool relies on local infrastructure. Local content cannot thrive without roads, electricity, warehouses, industrial zones, and efficient transport networks. The state must invest in the construction of special economic zones, logistics hubs, and technology centers in the country's key regions. This infrastructure forms the physical foundation of economic development. Its existence enables local producers to transport their goods to markets, reduces logistics costs, and improves the quality of locally processed products.

Finally, digitalization is an essential driver of modern development. Digital technology can connect producers and consumers, facilitate the marketing of local products, and give Congolese businesses national and international visibility. E-commerce platforms, traceability applications, and electronic payment systems can revolutionize traditional economic channels. The DRC, with its connected and creative youth, can make digital technology a cornerstone of local content and a tool for expanding its economic reach across the African continent.

These various instruments must be interconnected to form a coherent ecosystem where each link in the chain , production, processing, distribution, and consumption, reinforces the others. Only through this systemic approach can the DRC transform its potential into real and sustainable wealth.

1. Develop complete value chains in strategic sectors

The most effective strategy for promoting local content is to build integrated supply chains, in which each stage of production, extraction, processing, distribution, export – is carried out locally.

Mining sector

Example of a possible value chain in the mining sector:

1. Local extraction (national workforce).

2. Local transport (national logistics).

3. Local processing (refining, hydrometallurgy).

4. Industrial assembly (batteries, electronic components).

5. Export of finished products, and no longer of raw ores.

The DRC can become a key player in the global battery industry thanks to cobalt, lithium, copper and nickel.

Agricultural sector

Develop regional agro-industrial hubs:

- Kasai: processing of cassava, maize, peanuts.
- Ecuador: palm oil, cocoa, fish.
- North Kivu / Ituri: coffee, cocoa, processed fruits and vegetables.

Objective: to export processed products, never raw materials.

Digital sector

Digital technology is a natural accelerator of local content.

Strategies:

- Provincial incubators;
- Local data centers;
- Start-ups specializing in agricultural, financial and educational solutions;
- Tax incentives for local innovation.

Cultural sector

Congolese culture and local know-how represent a gigantic economic potential.

Congolese culture is not merely an intangible heritage; it is a major economic and identity-building force. In the local content strategy, culture and traditional know-how constitute essential pillars of endogenous development. Indeed, Congolese creative genius is expressed in music, dance, fashion, sculpture, painting, gastronomy, and numerous other art forms. These expressions, deeply rooted in the country's cultural diversity, reflect the vitality of the Congolese people and their capacity to innovate within their own traditions.

The cultural industry can become a true engine of growth. Congolese music, already internationally renowned, could generate even more revenue if production chains, recording studios, distribution platforms, local labels, festivals, were developed within the country. Congolese cinema, still emerging, deserves support from public and private investment to tell local stories, promote national values, and provide employment for young people. The great epics of kingdoms such as the Bushi kingdom, which encompassed the territories of Kabare, Walungu, Idjwi, Mwenga, Bukavu, and Kalehe ; the Kongo kingdom, with Nzinga Nkuvu; the Luba and Lunda empires of Ilunga Mbindi and Mwant Yav; and the history of the copper miners who practiced artisanal copper extraction and smelting as early as the 19th century, could be the subject of short or feature films conceived and directed by Congolese filmmakers.

As for the visual arts, they constitute an exceptional showcase for the image of Congo abroad. By promoting their professionalization, the State would contribute to creating a strong and economically viable cultural identity.

Tourism and handicrafts also represent considerable potential. Regions like Kasai, Kongo-Central, and Katanga are home to unique artisanal traditions, whether in sculpture, basketry, textiles, or jewelry. These skills, passed down from generation to generation, deserve to be promoted through the creation of tourist circuits, craft centers, and dedicated markets. Congolese handicrafts, if structured and supported by incentive policies, can become a significant source of income for local communities, while simultaneously strengthening the positive image of "Made in Congo."

Finally, local innovation must be grounded in the wisdom of traditions. Combining ancestral knowledge with modern technologies allows for the design of original and competitive products. For example, in the housing sector, Congolese architects are reinventing local materials to create ecological and climate-adapted buildings. In fashion, designers are merging traditional fabrics with contemporary design to conquer African markets. These examples demonstrate that Congolese creativity, when supported, can become an engine of exports and national pride. Local content, understood in this way, is not simply an economic policy: it is the living expression of Congolese identity and ingenuity.

Strategic actions to be taken within the framework of local content development in the cultural sphere:

- Sovereign wealth fund dedicated to culture;
- National House of Music;
- Congolese streaming platforms;
- Schools of modern art.

2. Congolese youth at the heart of development

The development of local content in the Democratic Republic of Congo relies first and foremost on its youth, who represent both the country's greatest resource and its greatest challenge. With over 60% of the population under the age of 25, the DRC possesses considerable human capital capable of driving a vision of autonomous and innovative development. However, this potential remains largely untapped due to a lack of adequate training, institutional support, and economic opportunities.

To unleash this potential, massive investment in technical and vocational training is essential. The education system must adapt to contemporary economic realities, emphasizing practical skills, innovation, and modern technologies. Modern vocational schools, industrial training centers, and digital learning programs must be established in every province. The goal is to train a generation of workers, technicians, and entrepreneurs capable of local production and processing.

Encouraging entrepreneurship is another essential lever. Young Congolese people are creative, ambitious, and full of ideas. What they often lack is not the will, but the resources. It is therefore crucial to open up access to funding, incubators, and public procurement opportunities. Initiatives such as innovation competitions, regional business incubators, and mentorship programs can catalyze this energy. Supporting young entrepreneurs means building a diversified and resilient economy.

Finally, youth civic participation must be encouraged. Internal development can only succeed if young people feel involved in nation-building. They must be included in shaping public policies, in economic councils, and in community programs. By involving young people in decision-making, the DRC can guarantee the continuity and sustainability of its local content policies.

In short, investing in Congolese youth is investing in the very future of the country. They are the driving force of change, the face of tomorrow's Congo, and the key to an economy that thrives on its own energy. By giving young people the necessary tools, skills, and confidence, the DRC will not only build strong local content, but above all, a development model based on dignity, creativity, and national autonomy.

Therefore, to get the best out of Congolese youth, massive training programs must be put in place:

- Modern technical schools;
- Partnerships with international universities;
- Sectoral centers of excellence (mining, energy, construction, digital)

3. Reduce dependence on outside help

For decades, the development of the DRC has been viewed through the lens of international aid. However, this dependence, often well-intentioned, has weakened the country's capacity to think and act independently. Reducing this dependence does not mean rejecting cooperation, but redefining it based on economic sovereignty. Congo must learn to be self-sufficient, to produce for itself, and to reinvest the fruits of its labor for the benefit of its people.

The first step is to create internal value chains. Too often, Congolese products leave the country unprocessed and return in a processed form, at a much higher price. This imbalance must be corrected by establishing integrated circuits: extraction, processing, marketing, and export must be controlled within the country. National companies must be encouraged to invest in local processing, with tax incentives and technical support. For example, in the mining sector, it is imperative to create industrial zones dedicated to manufacturing batteries and electronic components from Congolese cobalt and lithium.

Next, the DRC must mobilize its own financial resources. National savings, often underutilized, can become a powerful lever for development. Local banks, microfinance institutions, and sovereign wealth funds should be directed toward financing Congolese initiatives. Congolese citizens, whether living within the country or in the diaspora, must be encouraged to invest in the national economy. Instruments such as development bonds or citizen investment funds can strengthen popular participation in financing national progress.

Finally, regional cooperation in Africa represents a strategic alternative to external dependence. By developing intra-African trade, particularly through the African Continental Free Trade Area (ACFTA), the DRC can expand markets for its products while consolidating a united African market. Before expanding to other continents. An integrated economy among neighboring countries would stabilize trade, share infrastructure, and harmonize regulations. Congo must no longer see itself as an isolated country dependent on external powers, but as a driving force in an Africa that is developing on its own.

Reducing dependence on foreign aid is therefore not merely an economic imperative; it is a matter of national dignity. It requires a change of mentality: moving from a logic of assistance to one of responsibility, from discourse on poverty to the practice of productivity.

4. Public policies as a catalyst

No sustainable development can take root without a strategic, visionary, and proactive state. The Congolese government plays a crucial role in providing local content with a coherent policy framework, effective tools, and clear direction. The state must move beyond simply regulating local development to become a catalyst for domestic growth, ensuring the coherence of local initiatives and partnering with the private sector.

First, appropriate legislation is essential. Specific laws must protect local industries from unfair competition by imposing local production quotas in public procurement and major projects, particularly mining and oil projects. Local content clauses must be included in all contracts with foreign investors to ensure that labor, inputs, and services are sourced primarily from the Congolese economy.

Furthermore, economic infrastructure forms the physical foundation of all development. Roads, railways, ports, and electrical and digital networks are essential for connecting production areas to markets. The government must invest heavily in national infrastructure, not only to attract investors but also to connect provinces and reduce the logistical costs that hinder the competitiveness of local businesses.

Training and education represent another essential pillar. Public policies must promote the creation of technical schools, vocational training centers, and partnerships between universities and businesses. The goal is to train technicians, engineers, craftspeople, and entrepreneurs capable of meeting the needs of the Congolese market. Education must be considered a tool for economic sovereignty: a well-educated people is a free people.

Finally, the state must create clear economic incentives. This includes preferential loans for local SMEs, tax exemptions for companies that process Congolese resources locally, and targeted subsidies for research, innovation, and local production. A smart tax framework can direct capital toward strategic sectors and encourage domestic investment.

Thus, when the State fully assumes its role as the engine of development, it can transform the country's potential into a dynamic, inclusive, and sovereign economy. Local content then becomes the guiding principle of a societal project: that of a Congo strong in its citizens, proud of its products, and master of its own destiny.

5 Concrete Examples of Success in the DRC

Despite the numerous structural challenges facing the Democratic Republic of Congo, insufficient infrastructure, external dependence, and a weak industrial base and several local initiatives demonstrate that the path to endogenous development is not only possible but already underway. These successes, often modest in their beginnings, embody the Congolese people's ability to transform constraints into opportunities and create value from their own resources.

One of the most emblematic examples is that of the agribusiness sector in Kisangani, in Tshopo Province. Long dependent on imported goods, this region is experiencing an agricultural revival thanks to the local processing of cassava, maize, and other food crops. Local small and medium-sized enterprises have established modern production units capable of transforming these products into flour, chips, biscuits, or biofuel. This initiative, supported by farmers' cooperatives and a few national investors, has created numerous jobs, improved farmers' incomes, and stabilized prices in local markets. Moreover, it has demonstrated that it is possible to build a complete value chain, from production to processing, without relying on massive foreign investment. Kisangani is thus showing the way to a local economy, where wealth remains within the community and fuels circular development.

In Kinshasa, the capital, the dynamism of the digital sector also illustrates the rise of a new generation of entrepreneurs. Congolese tech startups are developing solutions tailored to the needs of the local market: mobile payment applications, e-commerce platforms, agricultural management tools, and digital educational solutions. Companies like Maxicash, Ingenious City, Congo Tech Network, and Schoolap embody this digital revolution made in Congo. Thanks to the ingenuity of young, locally trained engineers and developers, technology is becoming an engine of growth and a tool for sovereignty. These initiatives prove that Congolese youth don't need to wait for imported models to innovate: they possess the skills, creativity, and determination necessary to meet national challenges.

Another rapidly changing sector is local mining. While large multinationals still dominate, small and medium-sized Congolese enterprises are emerging, striving to process some of the extracted minerals locally. Some are already producing copper cathodes or cobalt ingots for regional markets. Others are partnering with universities to develop environmentally friendly processing methods. These efforts, though still limited, are paving the way for the gradual industrialization of the mining sector and greater retention of added value within the country.

These experiences demonstrate that the country possesses a productive energy that simply needs to be supported and amplified. They also prove that the success of domestic development depends less on foreign capital than on national will, good governance, and synergy among local actors: producers, entrepreneurs, researchers, public institutions, and communities. The success of these initiatives should inspire an ambitious national policy capable of replicating these models on a large scale in agriculture, industry, technology, and culture.

Adding to these numerous local entrepreneurial initiatives, the promulgation of Law No. 26/018 of June 30, 2026 on local content , supported by an ambitious National Local Content Plan, appropriate regulatory measures and rigorous governance , is likely to accelerate poverty reduction, promote the emergence of a genuine middle class, create national champions capable of driving the country's industrialization and, more broadly, establish the economic sovereignty of the Democratic Republic of Congo.

6. Lessons learned from personal experience as an entrepreneur

I entered entrepreneurship at a very young age, initially in the private sector, even before holding public office. My beginnings were marked by several structural obstacles specific to the Congolese context: the lack of accessible financing, the absence of support for young entrepreneurs, and a market dominated by very powerful foreign players.

After several years spent in South Africa, Zimbabwe, Zambia, and Mozambique, I acquired an international perspective on business and development. Returning to invest in the DRC was a courageous but strategic choice : I deeply believed in the potential of my country.

In my early years, I worked in various sectors, mining, energy, industry, and the supply of goods and services. This allowed me to understand the real needs of the market and to learn how to structure companies capable of lasting.

61. Decisive Choices

The decisive choices were:

- to surround myself with competent teams,
- secure strong partnerships,
- systematically reinvest in growth,
- and maintain an impeccable work ethic, even when shortcuts seemed tempting.

Significant successes are not only financial. I am proud to have contributed to creating local employment, training and mentoring young professionals, and above all to have demonstrated that Congolese entrepreneurship can be rigorous, visionary and international in scope.

62. Entrepreneurial Culture

Creating a strong entrepreneurial culture requires acting simultaneously on four pillars :

1. Education

Integrate entrepreneurship into schools, universities, and training centers. Young people must be trained in innovation, management, discipline, and calculated risk-taking.

2. Support

Incubators, mentors, specialized programs… Young entrepreneurs need guidance, not just talk.

3. The environment

For young people to create, we need:

- a simple administrative framework,
- clear public policies,
- real access to financing,
- protection of local production.

An enterprising youth is not a coincidence: it is the result of an ecosystem designed for them.

4. Discipline

Entrepreneurial spirit cannot thrive sustainably without a culture of discipline, founded on respect for laws, contractual commitments, business ethics, quality, and punctuality. Developing this culture requires promoting, from a young age, the values of a job well done, responsibility, integrity, and perseverance. A competitive economy does not relies not only on talent or resources, but also on individual and collective discipline which inspires investor confidence, strengthens corporate credibility and promotes sustainable growth.

63. Major constraints encountered

1. The difficulty of financing

I had to use self-financing, reinvestment of profits, and private partnerships. This taught me to start small but think big.

2. Administrative burdens

I chose the path of total compliance. It takes longer at the beginning, but it creates lasting credibility.

3. The business climate

I have always favoured transparency, collaboration with the State and the formalisation of activities.

4. Lack of infrastructure

This requires planning, maintaining high standards, and creativity in execution.

5. The lack of local expertise in certain sectors

I have invested in training, skills transfer and the promotion of Congolese talent.

64. As Director General of ARSP (2022-2026)

During my time at ARSP from November 2022 to June 2026, I focused my mandate on a clear objective: to make the law on subcontracting a real lever for the development of the Congolese private sector. Key actions were carried out in the areas of local content and subcontracting.

1. Sanitation of the sector

- Identification and elimination of fictitious or non-compliant companies;

- Implementation of a strict control system in all provinces.

2. Promotion of local content
- Implementation of national and sectoral local content policies with businesses and the population. Indeed, the ARSP is responsible in particular for the design, implementation and monitoring and evaluation of the national and sectoral local content policy in accordance with Decree No. 18/019 of May 24, 2018 establishing, organizing and operating the ARSP as

amended and supplemented to date by Decree No. 20/025 of October 12, 2020;

- Provincial tours of mines and industries to enforce compliance with legislation relating to subcontracting.

3. Strengthening local competitiveness

- Supporting local SMEs and other eligible companies in accessing subcontracting markets.

4. Audits of multinational corporations

Regular checks were carried out to verify:

- Compliance with subcontracting legislation,
- Access for eligible entrepreneurs to subcontracting markets in the private sector,
- Transparency and fairness in the awarding of said contracts.

5. International influence

Participation, to defend the Congolese vision of local content, in international forums such as INDABA MINING in Cape Town , South Africa, under the patronage of Congolese President Félix Tshisekedi and South African President Cyril Ramaphosa in February 2023; PDAC in March 2024 in Toronto, Canada; China-Africa Summit in September 2024 in Beijing, China, under the auspices of President Xi Jinping, as well as the China-DRC forum under the high patronage of President Tshisekedi ; meeting with His Highness Sheikh Saud bin Saqr Al Qasimi , in Ras Al Khaimah (United Arab Emirates) on the sidelines of the Global Citizen Forum held from December 4 to 5, 2024; US-DRC Economic Forum in Washington, DC, in October 2025, organized by the Presidency of the Democratic Republic of Congo.

International recognition with the FORBES USA award in 2024 among the ten best African managers of the year.

Despite these major advances, difficulties have been encountered in implementing local content. These difficulties include:

(i) The resistance of certain multinationals

Some international players are finding it difficult to accept the new rules.

(ii) The weak structure of some Congolese businesses. They need support to become more competitive.

(iii) Political and economic pressures. Any profound reform disturbs certain established interests.

(iv) The data gap. Creating a reliable statistical system is a national challenge.

(v) Inter-institutional coordination. The implementation of local content policies requires inter-institutional coordination: Ministries of Portfolio, Mines, Infrastructure, Transport, Hydrocarbons, Energy, PTNTIC, Industry, SMEs, ARSP, and all structures within the entrepreneurial ecosystem, as well as employers' organizations in the private sector. Synchronization is not always seamless.

President FELIX-ANTOINE TSHISEKEDI's vision of creating a strong Congolese middle class through local entrepreneurship and his unwavering support has legitimized all the actions I have taken in implementing the Law on Subcontracting as well as national and sectoral policies on local content.

Photos and illustrative images

LUBUMBASHI 2012

Johannesburg 2013: Signing of the agreement on the construction of the HDPE piping plant in the DRC

IN 2014: Agreement with the company MBS on transport between South Africa and the DRC

2014 signatures for the purchase of sulfuric acids

With Robert Friedland

With George Arthur Forrest

With Kurt house

With The CEO of CMOC Group

With Barrick Group

Speaker at Indaba Mining 2025 (RSA)

Speaking at the CODES conference in Kinshasa

Speaking at the MINING TECH conference in Kolwezi

Speaker at the US/DRC Economic Investment Forum

DRC-China Economic Forum

Speaker at the DRC MINING WEEK EXPO & CONFERENCE

Speaker at the Conference at the University of Mbuji-mayi

Speaking at the Conference of the Belgian-Congolese-Luxembourg Chamber of Commerce

Speaker at the Entrepreneurs' Conference in Central Kongo

Speaker at PDAC/CANADA 2024

DRC/USA Economic Forum 2025

Signing of the ARSP/FEC Sectoral Guides

Memorandum of Understanding between ARSP and the Ministry of Mines

Memorandum of Understanding between ARSP and the Ministry of Infrastructure and Public Works

Memorandum of Understanding between ARSP and the Ministry of Employment, Labour and Social Welfare

ARSP/BEE Memorandum of Understanding

ARSP/ARPTC Memorandum of Understanding

ARSP/ONEM Memorandum of Understanding

ARSP/FEC Memorandum of Understanding

Compliance checks for subcontracting

Visit to the Kibali Gold company

Visit to Huawei company

Visit to the Bralima company

Coronation prime infra (2020)

Forbes 2024 Coronation Award (USA)

6. Access to financing

- Create a Congolese development bank with concessional credit lines for SMEs and startups;

- Strengthen the structures in charge of guarantee funds;

- Strengthen the synergy between the entrepreneurial ecosystem and the industry promotion fund (FPI).

7. Local Certification

A National Standardization Committee (CNN), chaired by the Secretary General for Industry, proposes the adoption of international standards as mandatory national standards, in accordance with Ministerial Decree No. CAB.MIN /IND/CNM/008/09/2020 of September 15, 2020, establishing technical committees tasked with reviewing international standards for specific products with a view to their adoption as Congolese national standards. The CNN has provided the Democratic Republic of Congo with a directory of 1,252 national standards (NCDs) covering various strategic sectors.

Congolese national standards (NCD) often adopt international standards (ISO, Codex Alimentarius) to facilitate foreign trade.

While the Congolese Office of Control (OCC) is the national body for standardization and conformity assessment. It is responsible for quality control, metrology and certification of local and imported products.

Compliance monitoring with Congolese industrial standards must be strengthened in order to develop "Made in Congo" labels. (cf. Decree No. CAB.MIN/IND/CJA/10/10/2020 of October 27, 2020 adopting Congolese national standards on cosmetic and detergent products, lubricants and petroleum products, cements, paints and varnishes, electrotechnics, information technology and security, road safety management and supply, sanitation, environment, wastewater and borehole water and their implementation).

8. Build suitable industrial and logistics infrastructure

Any local content strategy will be ineffective without strong infrastructure.

Special Economic Zones (SEZs)

Special economic zones (SEZs) must provide:

- reliable energy;
- logistics ;
- tax advantages;
- administrative facilitation.

Logistics corridors

Relate :

- mining areas to industrial areas;
- agricultural areas to urban markets;
- cities with ports.

Energy infrastructure

Without energy, no local content is possible.

9. Mobilizing the diaspora as a productive force

The Congolese diaspora is an untapped resource: engineers; doctors; researchers; entrepreneurs.

Strategies:

- Creation of a diaspora investor status;
- Development obligations;
- Industrial partnerships with Congolese people living abroad;
- Facilitating the temporary return of skills (technical mission programs).

10. Integrate technological innovations

Technology is an accelerator of endogenous development.

Examples:

- Agricultural drones;
- Artificial intelligence for mining monitoring;
- Blockchain to trace the origin of minerals;
- Fintechs to facilitate payments;
- Digital platforms for SME registration.

1.1 Make the education sector the heart of local content

No country can build local content without a strong education system.

Key actions:

- Complete revision of school curricula (orientation towards useful professions);
- Dual training (School-Company);
- Proliferation of technical or vocational schools in line with the potential of the provinces;
- Provincial vocational training centers.

12. Create an enabling legal and fiscal environment:

- mandatory local content clauses in all contracts;

- sanctions for non-compliant companies;

- tax advantages for local businesses;

- legal recognition of the "local producer".

13. Promote economic patriotism

Local content is not just a public policy.

It is also a culture.

We need to develop:

- National preference;
- The pride of Congolese products;
- Buy Congo" campaigns ;
- Education in economic citizenship.

14. Develop a digital ecosystem for tracking local content

Digitalization enables:

- Real-time monitoring of companies' obligations;
- Transparency in the awarding of contracts;
- Traceability of local suppliers;
- The fight against shell companies.

A National Portal for Local Content is essential.

15. National and provincial coordination

Local content must be applied to:

- National level (legal and regulatory framework);
- Provincial level (controls, training, SME development);
- Sectoral level (mining, energy, agriculture, ICT…)

16. Towards a virtuous circle

Promoting local content in the Democratic Republic of Congo goes beyond mere economic ambition; it is a choice of civilization and sovereignty. In a world where nations are redefining themselves by their capacity to produce, innovate, and feed themselves, the DRC must now rely on its own strengths. Its natural resources, dynamic youth, cultural diversity, and human capital constitute the pillars of sustainable and authentically Congolese development.

The goal is not to reject international trade, but to rebalance it based on a solid foundation: producing locally for local consumption, before exporting the surplus. This paradigm shift would allow the country to drastically reduce its dependence on imports and foreign aid, which have too often fostered a rentier economy instead of a production-based one. By strengthening its internal capacities, the DRC can build a resilient economy, less exposed to global fluctuations and more deeply rooted in its local realities.

Local content is also a driver of innovation and inclusion. By stimulating the creation of local businesses, it fosters economic diversification and job creation, particularly for young people. Every locally processed product, every service designed by a Congolese person, every business born from national expertise contributes to strengthening collective confidence and changing the country's narrative. Congo will no longer be perceived as a place of extraction, but as a hub of creation and transformation.

Beyond figures and policies, local content also touches on national pride. It reflects a fundamental idea: that of a people capable of taking charge of their own destiny, valuing their culture, developing their talents, and building their future. It is a profoundly political and civic approach, where the state, businesses, and civil society work together toward a shared vision: that of productive autonomy and national dignity.

The challenge is significant, but the direction is clear. If the Democratic Republic of Congo succeeds in consolidating the promotion of local content—through the implementation of the Local Content Law, supported by an ambitious National Local Content Plan, appropriate regulatory measures, and rigorous governance —it will be able to set in motion a virtuous cycle :

- produce what it consumes,
- transform what it extracts,
- export what it has mastered,
- and reinvest what she earns.

Thus, the country will transition from being a supplier of raw materials to a producer of added value. Development will no longer come from outside, but from the very heart of Congo, driven by its men, women, and youth.

The DRC can then become an African model of endogenous development, a country where wealth is no longer extracted but created, where sovereignty is no longer a dream but a practice, and where local content becomes the engine of a modern, innovative and inclusive economy.

Conclusion

The final chapter focused on tools for local content development.

Promoting local content in the DRC must be based on a coherent set of economic, financial, institutional and technological tools capable of supporting private initiative, stimulating production and ensuring the competitiveness of Congolese products on the national and African markets.

Among the tools I mentioned were financial instruments to create an environment where Congolese entrepreneurs, artisans, farmers and innovators can access financing on favorable terms.

The State, through the newly established Development Bank of Congo and partner institutions, is called upon to provide support funds for SMEs, low-interest loans for local projects, and targeted subsidies. Furthermore, strategic partnerships are essential to strengthen scientific research, modernize production tools, and open markets for Congolese products.

We need to promote local infrastructure and digitalization. Digital technology makes it possible to connect producers to consumers, facilitate the marketing of local products and give national and international visibility to Congolese companies.

I propose developing complete value chains in strategic sectors and building integrated sectors that encompass mining, agriculture, digital technology, culture (Congolese music, cinema, the great epics of ancient kingdoms and empires), visual arts, tourism, and crafts. Congolese youth must be placed at the heart of development through technical and vocational training, entrepreneurship, and civic participation.

It is imperative to reduce dependence on external aid, which is a matter of national dignity that requires a shift from a logic of assistance to one of responsibility.

I propose promoting regional cooperation in Africa. Public policies must become a catalyst for the development of local content through appropriate legislation and specific laws that protect local industries against unfair competition.

Economic infrastructure is needed, the physical foundation of all development (roads, railways, ports, electrical and digital networks are essential).

The state must facilitate economic incentives: preferential loans for local businesses, tax exemptions for companies that process Congolese resources locally. This requires national will, good governance, and synergy among local stakeholders: producers, entrepreneurs, researchers, public institutions, and communities.

As I have emphasized, promoting local content in the Democratic Republic of Congo is a matter of civilization and sovereignty. For its sustainable development, the DRC must value its natural resources, its dynamic youth, its cultural diversity, and its human capital. We must produce locally to consume locally, before exporting any surplus.

Local content is also a driver of innovation and inclusion. It speaks to national pride and embodies the idea of a people capable of taking charge of their own destiny, valuing their culture, developing their talents, and building their future. It represents a commitment to productive autonomy and national dignity.

Despite the challenges, the path forward is now clearly defined. The effective implementation of the Local Content Law can be a powerful driver of economic growth, the emergence of a genuine Congolese middle class, and the creation of national champions.

General Conclusion

Africa is at a crossroads. It bears both the weight of its history and the promise of its future. While previous generations fought for political freedom, the current generation must lead the fight for economic sovereignty. This fight, the fight for the continent's development through local content, or simply the fight to return economic power to the people, cannot be won through rhetoric or indignation, but through the gradual and determined construction of robust production systems, rooted in local realities and structured around a clear vision: transforming African resources into African wealth, for Africans.

My investigation was structured around six chapters. The first focused on the current situation in Africa and the challenges of development. I discussed the impact of globalization on local industries in Africa, resulting in a globalized economy that leads to mixed feelings: Afro-pessimism for some, hope for others. The challenges to Africa's development include education, unemployment, economic growth, poverty and inequality, governance and institutions, climate change, and the environment. Examples from specific countries illustrated my points.

The second chapter focused on the challenges to the efficient implementation of local content development policies, including a lack of technical and technological capacity, inadequate infrastructure, limited access to financing, international competition, a complex regulatory and administrative framework, weak local demand, and the need to strengthen local capacities. Promoting local content is essential for its effective development. Internal capacity building through training and workshops, coaching and mentoring, targeted recruitment of freelancers and new talent, diversification of financial instruments, improvement of the business environment, use of digital technology, support from public authorities, strengthening of cooperation. Regulatory reforms, simplification of procedures, good governance, strategic partnerships.

The third chapter focused on the institutional framework and the roles of stakeholders in the implementation of sectoral and national policies for local content development in the Democratic Republic of Congo. Regarding local content and the reform of the institutional framework, it seemed appropriate to mention the Entrepreneurship Guarantee Fund in Congo (FOGEC), the National Agency for the Development of Congolese Entrepreneurship (ANADEC), the Agency for the Promotion of the Middle Classes (APROCM), the Regulatory Authority for Subcontracting in the Private Sector (ARSP), and to recall the promulgation of Law No. 26/018 of June 30, 2026, on Local Content in the Democratic Republic of Congo, which entrusts the regulation of local content in the private sector to the ARSP and that in the public sector , specifically public procurement and public-private partnerships, to the Public Procurement Regulatory Authority (ARMP). Regarding stakeholders, I reiterated the role of specialized agencies in regulation and control, as well as the roles of multinational corporations, local SMEs, universities, research centers, local communities, civil society, the media, the diaspora, and inter-institutional coordination.

The strategies to be implemented for the promotion of local content in Africa, using the Democratic Republic of Congo as an example, were the subject of the fourth chapter. Faced with the Democratic Republic of Congo's population growth, coupled with pessimistic forecasts for its development and major challenges for young people regarding employment, housing, and education, I am convinced that only the promotion of local content remains an opportunity and an economic, cultural, and strategic imperative for the emergence of the continent and the Democratic Republic of Congo. This requires government ambitions aligned with national development plans and *political and regulatory frameworks,* support for Congolese entrepreneurship, training and skills development for local communities, political leadership, and a national consensus among the State, public and private companies, civil society, universities, research centers, and local authorities. In addition to the provisions already included in the Local Content Law, the establishment of a dedicated financing system for content , including the creation of a National Fund for the Promotion of Local Content (FNPCL), a national training and skills transfer program, I propose the creation of a National Directory of Local Suppliers and Service Providers, the establishment of "industrial clusters" in the provinces and innovative financial instruments). I support the promotion of "Made in Congo", the national culture of buying local through national awareness campaigns " Buy Congo, Build Congo" "Our resources, our wealth" "Congo produces, Congo consumes".

The proposals formulated in this chapter constitute guidelines that may enrich the development of the National Local Content Plan.

In the fifth chapter, I felt it appropriate to discuss the principles and mandatory guidelines for implementing sectoral and national local content development policies in the Democratic Republic of Congo. As essential steps in developing local content policies, I proposed ensuring compatibility with national development objectives, assessing the current situation, developing local content policies, and monitoring, reviewing, and implementing them. The principles to be respected include protecting the business climate, strengthening the national private sector, transparency, building the capacity of local content implementation institutions, mutual cooperation among stakeholders, promoting women and youth, and protecting people with disabilities. I supported the idea of mandatory procurement of goods and services from local suppliers, employment and investment in staff training, partnerships between foreign and national companies for technology and skills transfer, and adding value to raw materials at the national level before export. In short, it concerns policies relating to supply, direct employment and local capital.

The need for a coherent set of economic, financial, institutional, and technological tools for developing local content in the Democratic Republic of Congo and Africa was addressed in the last chapter. It is desirable that the State, through the Development Bank of Congo (to be established) and partner institutions, make support funds available to local businesses, provide preferential loans for local projects, and offer targeted subsidies. Strategic partnerships, local infrastructure, and digitalization, enabling digital technologies to connect producers and consumers, are essential. It is necessary to promote value chains in strategic sectors and build integrated value chains that encompass the mining, agricultural, digital, and cultural sectors. Congolese youth must be placed at the heart of development through technical and vocational training, entrepreneurship, and civic participation. Economic infrastructure is crucial, as it forms the foundation of all development (roads, railways, ports, and electrical and digital networks are essential). The government is urged to facilitate economic incentives: preferential loans for local SMEs, and tax exemptions for companies that process Congolese resources locally. National commitment, good governance, and synergy among local stakeholders (producers, entrepreneurs, researchers, public institutions, and communities) are essential.

Throughout this work, we have explored the structural issues, institutional challenges, international examples, multiple obstacles, and pragmatic strategies needed to make local content a true lever for transformation.

The diagnosis is unequivocal: without a coordinated, demanding, and disciplined effort in training, governance, financing, technology, and strengthening the entrepreneurial fabric, the continent will continue to circle its potential without ever fully realizing it. Local content should not be seen as a defensive measure against multinationals, but as a comprehensive societal project that engages states, the private sector, the population, educational institutions, and international partners. It embodies a strategic vision: to integrate African youth into global value chains, to give local businesses a central role, and to enable African nations to participate, not simply as suppliers of raw materials, but as creators of value, in the global economy. For this dream to materialize, several conditions must be met:

1. A firm and sustainable political vision, driven by a leadership aware that economic sovereignty is built on consistency,

exemplary conduct and rigor with the ultimate goal of returning economic power to the people;

2. A collective discipline, a profound cultural transformation that puts work well done, continuous learning and individual responsibility at the center of nation-building;

3. Transparent, modern and coordinated governance, where the State, architect and shield of local content, fully plays its role by putting in place clear and applicable laws; where accountability and inter-institutional collaboration becomes the norm and not the exception, and where trust between institutions and citizens is rebuilt;

4. A massive investment in human capital, because Africa will not be developed until its children are educated, qualified and valued;

5. Smart industrialization, based on strategic sectors, technology, and the construction of integrated value chains;

6. A balanced partnership with the rest of the world, where Africa negotiates on an equal footing, strong in its vision, strong in its capabilities, strong in its institutions;

Developing a prosperous Africa through local content is not a naive dream. It is a realistic ambition, fueled by the history of nations that, starting from less disadvantaged positions than the African continent, have managed to transform constraints into opportunities and poverty into strength. It is an ambition driven by a clear-sighted African generation, aware of the challenges but resolutely committed to action.

This prosperity will not be built in a day. It will take time, demand sacrifices, require discipline, perseverance, and the courage to confront both internal and external resistance. But it is possible. It is necessary. It is inevitable if Africa is to occupy the place that history has reserved for it.

In conclusion, we can affirm that Africa's future belongs to those who can transform its potential into real power by leveraging collective intelligence, productive work, responsible governance, and the deep integration of local content into public policies and private practices. It is through this path that Africa will write its own economic history, free itself from past dependencies, and make its unique contribution to the human adventure.

The dream of our fathers then becomes more than an inheritance: it becomes a project. A project for today, for tomorrow, and for the generations to come. A project that Africa, at last, is ready to realize.

My final point is that promoting local content in the Democratic Republic of Congo and across Africa is a matter of civilization and sovereignty. For its sustainable development, the country must value its natural resources, its dynamic youth, its cultural diversity, and its human capital. We must produce locally to consume locally, before exporting any surplus.

Local content is also a driver of innovation and inclusion. It speaks to national pride and embodies the idea of a people capable of taking charge of their own destiny, valuing their culture, developing their talents, and building their future. It represents a commitment to productive autonomy and national dignity.

Therefore, promoting local content is not merely an economic issue; it represents a genuine strategic lever for the country's sovereignty, resilience, national pride, and long-term prosperity. Reducing dependence on foreign aid is an act of national dignity that implies a shift from a logic of assistance to one of responsibility.

Partial bibliography

1. AFRICAN UNION (AU) (2022). *Report on the Sustainable Development Goals in Africa.* Addis Ababa: AU Commission.

2. Barack Obama (2009). *Speech at the University of Ghana,* Accra, July 11, 2009. Official text available in the White House archives.

3. CENTRAL BANK OF RUSSIA / *historical documents on the war in Ukraine*

4. General Historical References on African revolts against forced labor: Boahen, AA (1987). *African Perspectives on Colonialism. Baltimore:* Johns Hopkins University Press.

5. IGF – *Extractive Sector Governance Initiative.* (2018). Local Content Policies in the Mining Sector: Case Studies and Lessons Learned. Ottawa: IGF Secretariat.

6. INTERNATIONAL LABOUR ORGANIZATION (ILO) (2023). *Employment Outlook and Trends in Sub-Saharan Africa.* Geneva: ILO.

7. Jean ORTIZ & Georges Fournial ORTIZ, (1999). *Cuba: The revolution in education.* Paris: Le Temps des Cerises.

8. Julien WAGNER, J. (2013). *China–Africa: The Great Plunder. Chinese Dream, African Nightmare* ? Paris: Éditions du Moment.

9. Marc PILON, M. (2004). *Challenges of development in sub-Saharan Africa: Education at stake.* Paris: Institute of Research for Development (IRD).

10. NATURAL RESOURCE GOVERNANCE INSTITUTE (NRGI) NRGI. (2020). *Local Content: Strengthening Governance and Economic Impact in Resource-Rich Countries.* New York: NRGI.

11. Nicolas SARKOZY (2007). *Dakar speech,* July 26, 2007. Official text of the speech reproduced in the archives of the French Presidency.

12. Nicole GNESOTTO & Giovanni GREVI (2007). *The World in 2025: A Brief History of the Future.* Paris: Robert Laffont. (Cited for the Afro-pessimistic and Afro-optimistic scenarios).

13. Pascal LAMY (2007). Preface. In N. Gnesotto & G. Grevi, *the World in 2025: A Brief History of the Future.* Paris: Robert Laffont.

14. REPUBLIC OF THE CONGO – *Local Legislation Republic of the Congo.* (1994). Hydrocarbons Code, Law of August 23, 1994. Republic of the Congo. (2000). Law No. 3-2000 of February 1, 2000, relating to subcontracting. Republic of the Congo. (2000). Decree No. 2000-180 of August 7, 2000, regulating subcontracting in the sector. Guinea. (2024). Law L-2024-013-CNT relating to Local Content in the Republic of Guinea.

15. Thomas L. FRIEDMAN, T. L. (2008). *Hot, Flat, and Crowded: Why We Need a Green Revolution, and How It Can Renew America* . New York: Farrar, Straus and Giroux. (Cited for its analysis of the "Chinese dream" requiring "another planet").

16. UNITED NATIONS DEVELOPMENT PROGRAMME (UNDP) (2023). *Human Development Report 2023.* New York: UNDP. (Cited for statistics on HDI, employment and life expectancy).

17. WORLD BANK (2023). *World Development Indicators.* Washington, DC: World Bank. (Regarding African growth, infrastructure, and poverty statistics).

Postface

Nana Addo Dankwa Akufo -Addo, Honorary President of the Republic of Ghana (2017-2025)

REPUBLIC OF GHANA

Nana Addo Dankwa Akufo-Addo

FORMER PRESIDENT OF THE REPUBLIC OF GHANA

For generations, the global economic architecture has viewed the African continent and the Democratic Republic of Congo in particular, through a highly restrictive lens: as a warehouse for raw material extraction. We have historically exported our crude oil, unrefined gold and strategic minerals to power foreign industrial revolutions, while our own communities bore the environmental and economic weight of depletion.

This structural imbalance has long meant that the real financial value, the specialized jobs and the industrial multiplier effects of African resources were captured overseas, leaving our citizens with the bare minimum.

This book arrives at a critical juncture in Africa's history. It goes beyond merely documenting our continent's historical challenges to offer practical, operational paths forward. Local content is no longer a peripheral policy option or a protectionist talking point. It is the defining frontline of African economic sovereignty.

The author's focus on the Democratic Republic of Congo is highly strategic. The DRC sits at the very heart of the global green energy transition. The planet's future from electric vehicles to advanced microchip, relies fundamentally on the cobalt, copper, lithium and coltan buried beneath Congolese soil.

Yet, as this book underscores, global technological progress cannot come at the expense of Congolese development. The historical tragedies of the past must not repeat themselves in the green era. True development in the DRC cannot be measured by the mere volume of raw ore shipped from its ports. It must be measured by the number of Congolese engineers trained, the domestic supply chains fortified, and the processing plants established right within the country. Without aggressive, well-enforced local content legal frameworks, resource wealth will continue to yield external growth for others instead of shared domestic prosperity for Africans.

the political, corporate and civil leadership of this continent to summon the collective resolve to act. Our most valuable resource is not the gold in our rocks, the oil in our oceans or the cobalt in our soil. It is the unyielding genius of our youth. Local content is the economic bridge that connects our natural wealth to our human potential. Let this book serve as a turning point where Africa permanently stops fueling the industrialization of others and begins, decisively, to manufacture its own future.

Personal Dedication

To the Author, Monsieur Miguel Kashal Katemb

It is one thing to observe the economic challenges of our continent from afar, but it is a far greater endeavour to provide our leadership with the intellectual playbook required to confront them. Your rigorous scholarship and unyielding commitment to Africa's structural transformation shine through every page of this work. You have not merely written a book; you have advanced a profound cause. For your dedication to our shared continental destiny and for giving clarity to the path ahead, you have my deepest gratitude and highest commendation.

Nana Addo Dankwa Akufo-Addo
President of the Republic of Ghana
(2017 – 2025)

Africa today stands at a pivotal moment in its economic history. As geopolitical and technological transformations reshape global balances, our continent is called upon to play a decisive role in the global economy, particularly due to its strategic natural resources, dynamic demography, and immense entrepreneurial potential.

The book *"The Development of Africa Through Local Content: The Case of the Democratic Republic of the Congo"* makes a significant contribution to the fundamental reflection on how Africa can transform its natural wealth into sustainable prosperity for its people.

The author highlights a reality long known to African nations: the possession of abundant natural resources does not automatically guarantee development. The economic history of our continent demonstrates that, too often, these resources have been extracted without generating structural transformation in our economies.

It is precisely in this context that the issue of local content becomes crucial. Local content is not merely a sectoral economic policy; it is a strategic instrument for industrial development, job creation, and the strengthening of national capacities.

The Ghanaian experience shows that industrialization, investment in local skills, and the active participation of national enterprises in value chains are essential elements for building an inclusive and sustainable economy. Public policies must encourage innovation, support African entrepreneurs, and create an environment conducive to productive investment.

The Democratic Republic of the Congo, with its immense mineral resources and considerable human potential, possesses the assets necessary to become one of the major hubs of industrial transformation on the African continent. However, to achieve this objective, it is essential that the exploitation of natural resources be accompanied by a coherent strategy of local transformation, skills transfer, and increased participation of national economic actors.

As the author demonstrates, the development of local content represents a promising pathway to reduce social inequalities, strengthen economic sovereignty, and promote inclusive growth. It also helps consolidate the foundations of a more resilient African economy capable of withstanding fluctuations in international markets.

Beyond the Congolese case, this work raises questions that concern the entire continent: how can Africa better leverage its resources? How can we build economies capable of creating jobs for our youth? How can natural wealth be transformed into social wealth?

These questions lie at the heart of Africa's development agenda and the ambitions carried by continental initiatives for economic transformation.

I commend the intellectual and patriotic commitment of the author, whose reflection invites policymakers, entrepreneurs, and African citizens to rethink the foundations of the continent's economic development.

May this work foster constructive debate for the whole of Africa.

Nana Akufo Addo
Former President of the Republic Ghana

Appendix: Comments

1 Dr. Edem Adzogenu, CEO of AfroChampions

At a time when Africa is seeking new pathways to economic sovereignty, Miguel Kashal Katemb offers a timely and thought-provoking examination of local content as a driver of industrial development, entrepreneurship, and national value creation. Grounded in the experience of the Democratic Republic of Congo but relevant across the continent, this book provides important insights into how African countries can strengthen domestic capabilities and build more inclusive and resilient economies. It is a valuable contribution to the growing discourse on economic sovereignty and Africa's long-term development.

Dr. Edem Adzogenu
Co-Chair, AfroChampions

2. Pascal Kinduelo Lumbu , Congolese businessman and senator (DRC)

Having dedicated a large part of my life to business, finance, credit, and the sometimes harsh realities of the market, I've come to a firm conviction: no nation can build lasting prosperity without its own entrepreneurs. This fundamental truth is brought to light by Miguel Kashal 's book. Katemb , The development of Africa through local content: the case of the Democratic Republic of Congo , by posing truths that are sometimes difficult to hear, but essential for the economic future of our African states.

A country's wealth is not measured solely by its natural resources or public revenues. It is measured above all by its capacity to foster women and men capable of producing, investing, transforming, and creating value within their own borders.

For a long time in the Democratic Republic of Congo, entrepreneurship evolved in a poorly structured, unregulated, and sometimes unprotected environment. Many Congolese initiatives survived with difficulty, facing a lack of adequate financing, weak institutional support, unfair competition, and a legal framework that was often insufficient to support their growth.

Yet the potential has always been there: Congolese entrepreneurial genius exists; it lives in our markets, in our workshops, in our farms, in our SMEs, in our crafts and in this youth who, every day, invent solutions despite the constraints.

What was often lacking was a structured vision to organize this energy.

Kashal 's book Katemb, sincerely deserve to be praised.

With the promulgation of Ordinance-Law No. 22/030 on the promotion of entrepreneurship and startups, and Ordinance -Law No. 22/031 on handicrafts, the DRC has begun to recognize more clearly that entrepreneurship and the organized informal economy are not marginal realities, but pillars of national development. These texts reflect a significant political will: to integrate and structure sectors that have long been neglected.

In the same vein, Law No. 17/001 of February 8, 2017, establishing the rules applicable to subcontracting in the private sector, introduced a strategic shift. It reflects a clear ambition: to foster the emergence of a genuine Congolese middle class by granting Congolese citizens access to private sector markets, which until then had been dominated by foreign interests or front companies.

Kashal 's work comes in. Katemb's work takes on its full meaning. This book is not merely an analytical work; it is a work of clear-sightedness. It poses the real questions, those that any serious economy must confront: how to protect without confining? How to promote nationals without weakening competitiveness? How to transform our resources into sustainable wealth? How to build an economy that truly benefits the Congolese people?

And above all, it doesn't stop at diagnosis; it proposes concrete solutions. This is what makes this work so valuable: it highlights the weaknesses of the DRC's economic model, but it also offers realistic solutions for rebuilding the Republic.

One of the most important points is undoubtedly the discussion surrounding the draft law on local content. If this reform is successful, it could mark a historic milestone in the Congolese economy. For the real challenge, as the author emphasizes, is not simply to participate in the economy, but to create national champions, Congolese captains of industry capable of leading each strategic sector: mining, agriculture, energy, telecommunications, digital technology, logistics, and manufacturing.

A strong country is built with a strong private sector. And a strong private sector is not the product of spontaneity; it is built through law, institutional support, discipline, facilitated access to financing, intelligent protection, and a clear national vision brought to the highest levels of government.

The economic future of the DRC will largely depend on its ability to transform its immense potential into national productive power.

This book reminds us of a fundamental truth: Congolese economic independence begins when Congolese people themselves become the main actors in their own economy. This, in my view, is one of the great struggles of our generation.

By Pascal Kinduelo Lumbu
Senator of the Republic – Entrepreneur

Postface

Par Pascal Kinduelo Lumbu
Sénateur de la République – Entrepreneur

Lorsqu'on a consacré une grande partie de sa vie à l'entreprise, à la finance, au crédit et aux réalités parfois rudes du marché, j'ai fini par me faire une conviction : aucune nation ne peut bâtir durablement sa prospérité sans ses propres entrepreneurs. C'est cette vérité fondamentale que met en lumière l'ouvrage **de Miguel Kashal Katemb, *Le développement de l'Afrique au travers du contenu local : cas de la République démocratique du Congo***, en posant des vérités parfois difficiles à entendre, mais incontournables pour l'avenir économique de nos Etats Africains.

La richesse d'un pays ne se mesure pas uniquement à ses ressources naturelles ou à ses recettes publiques. Elle se mesure surtout à sa capacité à faire émerger des femmes et des hommes capables de produire, d'investir, de transformer et de créer de la valeur sur leur propre sol.

Pendant longtemps, en République démocratique du Congo, l'entrepreneuriat a évolué dans un environnement peu structuré, peu encadré et parfois peu protégé. Beaucoup d'initiatives congolaises ont survécu dans la difficulté, confrontées à l'absence de financement adapté, à la faiblesse de l'accompagnement institutionnel, à la concurrence déséquilibrée et à un cadre juridique souvent insuffisant pour soutenir leur croissance.

Pourtant, le potentiel a toujours été là : le génie entrepreneurial congolais existe ; il vit dans nos marchés, dans nos ateliers, dans nos fermes, dans nos PME, dans notre artisanat et dans cette jeunesse qui, chaque jour, invente des solutions malgré les contraintes.

Ce qui manquait souvent, c'était une vision structurée pour organiser cette énergie.

C'est pourquoi les actions et réformes engagées ces dernières années, sous la présidence de Felix TSHISEKEDI comme relevé dans l'ouvrage de Miguel Kashal Katemb, méritent sincèrement d'être saluées.

Avec la promulgation notamment, de l'**Ordonnance-Loi n°22/030 relative à la promotion de l'entrepreneuriat et des startups** et de l'**Ordonnance-Loi n°22/031 relative à l'artisanat**, la RDC a commencé à reconnaître, de manière plus claire, que l'entrepreneuriat et l'économie informelle organisée ne sont pas des réalités marginales, mais des piliers du développement national. Ces textes traduisent une volonté politique importante : celle d'intégrer et de structurer des secteurs longtemps laissés à eux-mêmes.

Dans la même dynamique, **la Loi n°17/001 du 08 février 2017 fixant les règles applicables à la sous-traitance dans le secteur privé** a introduit une rupture stratégique. Elle traduit une ambition claire : **faire émerger une véritable classe moyenne congolaise** à travers l'accès des nationaux aux marchés économiques du secteur privé jusque-là dominés par des intérêts extérieurs ou des structures de façade.

C'est là que l'ouvrage de Miguel Kashal Katemb prend tout son sens. Ce livre n'est pas seulement un travail d'analyse ; c'est un travail de lucidité. Il pose les vraies questions, celles que toute économie sérieuse doit affronter : comment protéger sans enfermer ? Comment promouvoir les nationaux sans affaiblir la compétitivité ? Comment transformer nos ressources en richesse durable ? Comment bâtir une économie qui profite réellement aux Congolais ?

Et surtout, il ne s'arrête pas au diagnostic, il propose des pistes concrètes. C'est ce qui fait la valeur de cet ouvrage : il met en lumière les faiblesses du modèle économique de la RDC, mais il offre aussi des solutions réalistes pour relever la République.

L'un des points les plus importants est sans doute la réflexion autour du **projet de loi sur le contenu local**. Si cette réforme aboutit, elle pourrait marquer une étape historique dans l'économie congolaise. Car le véritable enjeu, comme le souligne l'auteur, n'est pas seulement de participer à l'économie, mais de créer des champions nationaux, des capitaines d'industrie congolais capables de porter chaque secteur stratégique : mines, agriculture, énergie, télécommunications, numérique, logistique ou industrie.

Un pays fort se construit avec un secteur privé fort. Et un secteur privé fort n'est pas le produit de la spontanéité ; il se construit par la loi, par l'accompagnement institutionnel, par la discipline, par la facilitation d'accès au financement, par la protection intelligente et par une vision nationale claire portée au plus haut sommet de l'Etat.

L'avenir économique de la RDC dépendra largement de cette capacité à transformer son immense potentiel en puissance productive nationale.

Cet ouvrage nous rappelle une vérité fondamentale : l'indépendance économique congolaise commence lorsque les Congolais deviennent eux-mêmes les principaux acteurs de leur propre économie. C'est là, à mon sens, l'un des grands combats de notre génération.

Par Pascal Kinduelo Lumbu
Sénateur de la République – Entrepreneur

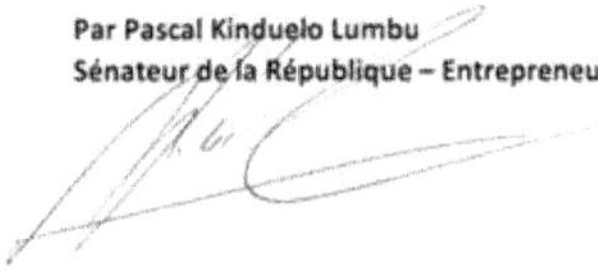

Table of Contents

Structures éditoriales du groupe L'Harmattan

L'Harmattan Italie
Via degli Artisti, 15
10124 Torino
harmattan.italia@gmail.com

L'Harmattan Hongrie
Kossuth l. u. 14-16.
1053 Budapest
harmattan@harmattan.hu

L'Harmattan Sénégal
10 VDN en face Mermoz
BP 45034 Dakar-Fann
senharmattan@gmail.com

L'Harmattan Cameroun
TSINGA/FECAFOOT
BP 11486 Yaoundé
inkoukam@gmail.com

L'Harmattan Burkina Faso
Achille Somé – tengnule@hotmail.fr

L'Harmattan Guinée
Almamya, rue KA 028 OKB Agency
BP 3470 Conakry
harmattanguinee@yahoo.fr

L'Harmattan RDC
185, avenue Nyangwe
Commune de Lingwala – Kinshasa
matangilamusadila@yahoo.fr

L'Harmattan Congo
67, boulevard Denis-Sassou-N'Guesso
BP 2874 Brazzaville
harmattan.congo@yahoo.fr

L'Harmattan Mali
ACI 2000 - Immeuble Mgr Jean Marie Cisse
Bureau 10
BP 145 Bamako-Mali
mali@harmattan.fr

L'Harmattan Togo
Djidjole – Lomé
Maison Amela
face EPP BATOME
ddamela@aol.com

L'Harmattan Côte d'Ivoire
Résidence Karl – Cité des Arts
Abidjan-Cocody
03 BP 1588 Abidjan
espace_harmattan.ci@hotmail.fr

Nos librairies en France

Librairie internationale
16, rue des Écoles
75005 Paris
librairie.internationale@harmattan.fr
01 40 46 79 11
www.librairieharmattan.com

Librairie des savoirs
21, rue des Écoles
75005 Paris
librairie.sh@harmattan.fr
01 46 34 13 71
www.librairieharmattansh.com

Librairie Le Lucernaire
53, rue Notre-Dame-des-Champs
75006 Paris
librairie@lucernaire.fr
01 42 22 67 13

www.ingramcontent.com/pod-product-compliance
Lightning Source LLC
LaVergne TN
LVHW050817061126
851857LV00012B/857
* 9 7 8 2 3 3 6 6 4 7 3 6 4 *